The LightFoot Companion to the via Francigena

Canterbury to the Great Saint Bernard Pass

3rd Edition

by
Babette Gallard

Copyright 2024 Pilgrimage Publications All rights reserved.

ISBN 978-2-917183-52-6

www.pilgrimagepublications.com

ALSO BY LIGHTFOOT GUIDES

LightFoot Guide to the via Francigena
    Canterbury to the Great Saint Bernard Pass, Switzerland
    The Great Saint Bernard Pass Switzerland to St Peter's, Rome, Italy

LightFoot Guide to the via Domitia, Arles to Vercelli

LightFoot Companion
    to the via Francigena - Italy
    to the Via Francigena - England, France and Switzerland
    to the via Domitia

LightFoot Guide to the Three Saints' Way
    Winchester to Mont St Michel
    Mont St Michel to St Jean d'Angely

LightFoot Guide to Foraging
    A guide to over 130 of the most common edible and medicinal plants in Western Europe

LightFoot Guide to the via Podiensis
    A complete guide to the 774 kilometre journey from Le Puy-en-Velay to the Pyrenees

Your Camino
    Information, maps for Camino routes in France and Spain

Camino Lingo
    A cheat's guide to speaking Spanish on the Camino

Slackpacking the Camino Frances
    All the information and advice you'll need to plan your perfect Camino

Author's note - A book of this type can be never complete. Feedback and suggestions are always welcomed. mail@pilgrimagepublications.com

For the latest guides visit www.pilgrimagepublications.com

With thanks to Jannina Veit Teuten for the cover image - Lausanne Cathedral watercolour www.jannina.net and to the many contributors to Wiki Commons for providing photos licensed and attributed under the Creative Commons Attribution-Share Alike 4.0 International license

Contents

Pilgrims and Pilgrimages	9
Labyrinth	10
The Via Francigena Yesterday and Today	11
A conduit for cultural and artistic change	12
Sigeric the Serious (990–994)	13
François-René de Chateaubriand	14

England 14

The County of Kent	16
The Aldington Gang	17
Canterbury	18
Canterbury Cathedral	19
Thomas Becket	20
Chaucer	20
The North Downs Way	21
Patrixbourne	22
Shepherdswell	23
The Green Man	23
Dover	23
Dover Castle	24
John Bunyan	25

France 27

The department of Pas-de Calais	29
Calais	29
Louis Blériot	30
Sangatte	31
Wissant	31
Sombre LXXX Sumeran	31
Jean-Pierre Blanchard	31
Guînes LXXVIII Gisne	33
Field of the Cloth of Gold	33
Wisques	34
Paul Vilain	35
Licques	36
Esquerdes	36
Thérouanne LXXVII Teranburh	37
The Siege of Thérouanne	38
Saint Audomar	38
Liettres	39
Amettes	39
Joseph Labre	39
Chaussée Brunehaut	40

Bruay la Buissière LXXVI Bruwaei	41
Courrières mine disaster	41
Ablain-Saint-Nazaire	42
Mont-Saint-Eloi Abbey Towers	42
Arras LXXV Atherats	43
Vauban	45
Bapaume	45
The department of The Somme	46
Joan of Arc	46
Péronne	48
Doingt LXXIV Duin	48
The Life of Gargantua and of Pantagruel	49
The Department of Aisne	50
Saint-Quentin	50
Saint Quentin, the saint	51
The Hundred Years War	52
Serancourt-le-Grand LXXIII Martinwaeth	54
Tergnier	54
Laon LXXII Mundlothuin	54
Premonstratensians	56
Abbey Vauclair	57
Corbeny LXXI Corbunei	57
The Department of Champagne	58
Reims LXX Rems	59
Clovis	62
Saint-Martin-sur-le-Pré	63
Châlons-en-Champagne LXIX Chateluns	63
Fontaine-sur-Coole LXVIII Funtaine	64
Via Agrippa	65
The Peutinger Map	65
Donnement LXVII Domaniant	65
The Department of Aube	65
Brienne-le-Chateau LXVI Breone	66
Napoleon Bonaparte	66
Bar-sur-Aube LXV Bar	67
Gaston Bachelard	67
The Department of Haute-Marne	67
The Goncourt brothers	68
Nicolas Camille Flammarion	69
Louise Michel	70
Clairvaux Abbey	71
St Bernard of Clairvaux	73
Chateauvillain	74

Blessonville LXIV Blaecuile	74
Humes LXIII Oisma	74
Langres	74
Denis Diderot (1713—1784)	75
Grenant LXII Grenant	76
The Department of Haute-Saône	76
Champlitte	76
Seveux LXI Sefui	77
The Antonine Itinerary	78
Cussey sur l'Ognon LX Cuscei	78
Besançon LIX Bysiceon	78
Notre-Dame des Buis	80
St Leonard	80
Ornans	81
Gustave Courbet	81
Mouthier-Haute-Pierre	82
The Department of Doubs	83
Nods LVIII Nos	83
Pontarlier LVII Punterlin	83
Victor Hugo	84
Absinthe	85
Pastis	85
Jougne LVI Antifern	86

Switzerland   *87*

Vaud	89
Orbe LV Urba	90
Lausanne LIV Losanna	91
Lord Byron	92
Charlie Chaplin	94
Vevey LIII Vivaec	96
Montreux	96
Valais	97
Aigle.....LII Burbulei	98
St Maurice-en-Valais LI Sce Maurici	98
St Maurice	99
Martigny	99
St Martin of Tours	100
Orsiéres L Ursiores	101
Bourg-st-Pierre XLIX Petrecastel	101
The Alpine Crossing of Hannibal	102
The Great-St-Bernard Pass	103

Next stop, Italy!!   *105*

Sigeric's Itinerary

LXXX	Sumeran	Sombre
LXXVIII	Gisne	Gulnes
LXXVII	Teranburh	Thérouanne
LXXVI	Bruwaei	Bruay-la-Buissière
LXXV	Atherats	Arras
LXXIV	Duin	Doingt
LXXIII	Martinwaeth	Seraucourt-le-Grand
LXXII	Mundlothuin	Laon
LXXI	Corbunei	Corbeny
LXX	Rems	Reims
LXIX	Chateluns	Chalons-en-Champagne
LXVIII	Funtaine	Fontaine sur Coole
LXVII	Domaniant	Donnement
LXVI	Breone	Brienne-le-Château
LXV	Bar	Bar-sur-Aube
LXIV	Blaecuile	Blessonville
LXIII	Oisma	Humes-Jorquenay
LXII	Grenant	Grenant
LXI	Sefui	Seveux
LX	Cuscei	Cussey-sur-l'Ognon
LIX	Bysiceon	Besancon
LVIII	Nos	Nods
LVII	Punterlin	Pontarlier
LVI	Antifern	Jougne
LV	Urba	Orbe
LIV	Losanna	Lausanne
LIII	Vivaec	Vevey
LII	Burbulei	Aigle
LI	Sce Maurici	Saint-Maurice
L	Ursiores	Orsières
XLIX	Petrecastel	Bourg-Saint-Pierre

The Pilgrimage

Give me my scallop-shell of quiet,
My staff of faith to walk upon,
My scrip of joy, immortal diet,
My bottle of salvation,
My gown of glory, hope's true gage;
And thus I'll take my pilgrimage.
Blood must be my body's balmer;
No other balm will there be given:
Whilst my soul, like quiet palmer,
Travelleth towards the land of heaven;
Over the silver mountains,
Where spring the nectar fountains;
There will I kiss
The bowl of bliss;
And drink mine everlasting fill
Upon every milken hill.
My soul will be a-dry before;
But, after, it will thirst no more.

Sir Walter Raleigh

Pilgrims and Pilgrimages

Pilgrim, a person who journeys to a sacred place, or a traveller or wanderer. Peregrini - those who go through fields (per agros), transients.

The epitome of the Medieval travelling man, the homo viator, was the pilgrim who embarked on a journey towards one of Christianity's holy destinations. The practice of peregrination was presented as an example of faith and charity, linked to the metaphor of our journey towards the ultimate spiritual and heavenly goal. The main destinations were Rome, Jerusalem and Santiago de Compostela, carried out on foot, with the help of nothing more than a 'burdon' - a term that originally referred to mules and later to the pilgrim staff. In addition, pilgrims wore a cloak, wide-brimmed hat and a haversack or purse around the waist.  Various illustrations and paintings depict a dressing ceremony with the bestowal of a blessing by the bishop before departure, but this was probably reserved for people of high rank. The Medieval sense of hospitality derives from a Christian concept of offering material and spiritual aid to one's fellow man. Hospitals were modelled on monastic settlements and existed as permanent religious institutions often run by monastic orders. The codes of behaviour and rules observed inside the institution also applied to the guests for the duration of their stay. Only the wealthier hospitals in towns and the most important institutions provided beds and food, while others restricted their hospitality to the primary necessities, straw to lie on and religious succour. In addition to the support provided by religious organisations, based on the concept of Misericordia (the Latin translation of the Hebrew word hesed, meaning loving-kindness), there were other hostels of a secular nature, such as inns and, in some cases, spas, but these were usually frequented by a wealthier clientèle, merchants and knights who carried money with them and also attracted brigands to such an extent that the municipal authorities were finally forced to intervene to protect all travellers, including the less wealthy pilgrims.

Labyrinth

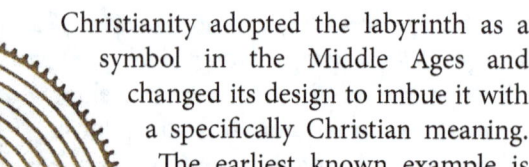

Christianity adopted the labyrinth as a symbol in the Middle Ages and changed its design to imbue it with a specifically Christian meaning. The earliest known example is from a 4th-century pavement in the Basilica of St Reparatus, Orleansville, Algeria, marked with the words Sancta Ecclesia at its centre, though it is unclear how it might have been used in worship. This movement was sustained until the 18th century when the essentially pagan origins of the labyrinth were recognised, and many were destroyed. Opinions as to the function and meaning of the old church labyrinths vary. Some maintain they were merely introduced as a symbol of the perplexities and intricacies of the Christian's path. Alternatively, it is asserted that the larger examples were used to perform miniature pilgrimages as a substitution for the long and arduous journeys. Some credence is given to this supposition by the name Chemin de Jérusalem, which is given to the vast labyrinth in Chartres cathedral. The accompanying ritual, supposedly involving pilgrims following the maze on their knees while praying, may have been practised there during the 17th century. The full flowering of the Medieval labyrinth came about from the 12th through to the 14th centuries with the grand pavement labyrinths of the Gothic cathedrals, notably Chartres, Reims and Amiens. The cathedral labyrinths inspire many turf mazes, such as those surviving at Wing, Hilton, Alkborough, and Saffron Walden in the United Kingdom.

LABYRINTHS ALONG THE VIA FRANCIGENA

Reims Cathedral, France
San Michele Maggiore, Pavia, Italy
San Pietro de Conflentu, Pontremoli, Italy
Lucca Cathedral, Italy

The Via Francigena Yesterday and Today

Omnes Via e Romam Perducunt' - All roads lead to Rome...

The Via Francigena is not a single road but a collection of several possible routes, which changed over the centuries as trade and the pilgrimage culture developed and also waned. Depending on the time of year, political situation, and relative popularity of the shrines of saints along the route, travellers may have used any of three or four crossings over the Alps and the Apennines. First documented as the Lombard Way and later the Iter Francorum, the Via Francigena was only mentioned as such in the Actum Clusi, a parchment produced in 876 in the Abbey of San Salvatore al Monte Amiata (Tuscany). Then, at the end of the 10th century, Sigeric the Serious, Archbishop of Canterbury, used the Via Francigena to travel to Rome for his consecration by the Pope. He recorded his return journey and the places where he stopped in a document now held in the British Library, but nothing in it suggests that the route was new. Sigeric's itinerary lists the seventy-nine submansiones which define the Via Francigena as we know it today. Many reports of journeys before and after Sigeric can only be apocryphal, but we can be certain that St Thierry, known as William of St Thierry, used the roads towards Rome on several occasions at the end of the 11th century. Other itineraries include those of the Icelandic traveller Nikolás Bergsson in 1154 and Philip Augustus of France, who entered Italy through Moncenisio in 1191. Subsequent accounts also cite the pass over Montgenévre and through the Susa Valley as a route used by pilgrims travelling to Rome (along what is now recognised as a branch of the Via Francigena) and armies invading Italy. In the 12th century, the increase in commercial relations between Italy and the Germanic areas led to a renewed use of the passes in the central and eastern Alps, such as the St Gotthard and Brenner passes. In the 13th century, trade grew to such an extent that several alternative routes to the Via Francigena were developed, and it consequently lost its unique character and broke into numerous routes linking the north to Rome. The walking paths and trails often linked monasteries instead of major cities, and by the 16th Century, there were more direct routes. Nevertheless, the Via Francigena route described by Sigeric was still in frequent use, as evidenced in the journey of Barthelemy Bonis, a merchant of Montauban who took part in the Jubilee of 1350, having survived the plague of 1348. Other documents also record Charles VIII's journey along the Via Francigena in 1494 as part of his armed descent on Naples. Today, the number of modern pilgrims on the Via Francigena is growing but still small compared to Medieval times, the heyday of long-distance pilgrimage in Europe. Since receiving the title of European Cultural Route from the Council of Europe in 1994, more resources and funds have been allocated to maintain, mark and promote the trail, particularly by the Italian Government. In 2007, a 0km milestone was laid outside Canterbury Cathedral, the official starting point. People who follow the Via Francigena can make of it what they will. A religious, spiritual, cerebral experience, a precious opportunity to discover Europe and the cultures along the route, a physical challenge, or all of the above, but they will be doing so with minimal environmental impact and hopefully a maximum understanding of the people they meet along the way.

A conduit for cultural and artistic change

The extent to which the Via Francigena facilitated all forms of exchange between communities is well known, one of the clearest examples being art and culture, or how else can we explain the vestment made from traditional Persian samite (a luxurious and heavy silk fabric often including gold or silver thread) dating back to the Carolingian age? Or the Codex Amiatinus, an 8th-century English Bible,  and the Vercelli Book left there by a Scotic pilgrim in the 6th century? Similarly, architects and builders were clearly open to the external influences brought in by the Via Francigena. Exchanges can be seen between the Lombard Romanesque style, or more generically, that of the Po region and France. A prime example of this can be found in the work of Nicolao, a sculptor who, between 1120 and 1140, was working on the abbey of San Michele della Chiusa in Piacenza, obviously inspired by the Wiligelmic tradition, but also by the art of the Aquitaine. In Tuscany, where French architectural styles are evident in buildings both along and near the Via Francigena, the abbey church of Sant'Antimo is the only one to have a basilica plan, complete with the aisle and side chapels typical of the great pilgrimage churches in France and Santiago de Compostela.

Sigeric the Serious (990–994)

Nothing in his history identifies Sigeric as being more serious than anyone else. The epithet may have originated from his learning or Serio, his translated name in Latin. Sigeric took holy orders at Glastonbury Abbey, where he was educated and subsequently elected Abbot of St Augustine's. In approximately 986, he was consecrated to the See of Ramsbury and Sonning and finally transferred to the See of Canterbury in 990. Today, Sigeric's main claim to fame is his journey from Rome to Canterbury. After receiving his cope and pallium (a circular band of white wool with pendants worn by archbishops) from the Pope, Sigeric recorded his return journey by listing the places he passed through and identifying them as 'submansiones', but he was also notable for several decisive acts for which future generations should be grateful. While Sigeric was an abbot, Ælfric dedicated a book of translated homilies to him and advised King Æthelred to found Cholsey Abbey in Berkshire in honour of King Edward the Martyr, as well as having Edward memorialized at Shaftesbury Abbey. Later, in 991, Sigeric advised King Æthelred to pay a tribute to the invading Danish king, Sweyn Forkbeard. Æthelred presented Sweyn with 10,000 pounds of silver, and in response, Sweyn temporarily ceased his destructive advance into England, though he did return later for a further tribute. Sweyn's ever-increasing demands in the following years resulted in a debilitating tax known as the Danegeld, payable by the inhabitants of Æthelred's territories. In 994, Sigeric paid tribute to the Danes and secured the protection of Canterbury Cathedral. Sigeric died on 28 October 994 and was buried in Christ Church, Canterbury. His Last Will and Testament left wall hangings to Glastonbury and a valuable collection of books for his church in Sonning.

François-René de Chateaubriand

"There never was a pilgrim who did not return to his village with one less prejudice and one more idea."

The French writer and historian set out from Paris in July 1806 - his ultimate goal, Jerusalem. On his return to France, he wrote the Itinéraire de Paris à Jérusalem, published in 1811 and described as the most widely-read book on Palestine in the early 19th century. The high point of Chateaubriand's pilgrimage was when he was made a knight of the Holy Sepulchre at the site of Christ's tomb with the sword of Godfrey of Bouillon. He described his motivation when he said: "I will perhaps be the last Frenchman leaving my country to voyage to the Holy Land with the ideas, feelings and aims of a pilgrim."

England

This royal throne of kings, this sceptred isle,
This earth of majesty, this seat of Mars,
This other Eden, demi-paradise,
This fortress built by Nature for herself
Against infection and the hand of war,
This happy breed of men, this little world,
This precious stone set in the silver sea,
Which serves it in the office of a wall,
Or as a moat defensive to a house,
Against the envy of less happier lands,
This blessed plot, this earth, this realm, this England ...
    William Shakespeare, John of Gaunt's speech from Richard II.

Your journey begins in England, the most populous part of the United Kingdom, bordered by Scotland, Wales, the Celtic Sea, the North Sea, and the English Channel. Although a relatively small country, England has held sway over almost every continent of the world at some time in history. This led to the spread of English people worldwide and the influx of other nations to this relatively small European island. With a story that stretches back more than 5000 years (and likely long before), England is a place where the past is a constant presence. Ruined castles perch on lonely hilltops. Mysterious menhirs (prehistoric standing stones), barrow tombs and stone circles sit in the corners of forgotten fields. Medieval cathedrals, regal palaces and improbably ostentatious stately homes pop up with bewildering regularity, and every English city, town and village has its own individual tale to tell. London is England's capital city and of the entire United Kingdom. It is ruled by a monarch, who uses parliament to manage the country through an elected Prime Minister. English cuisine has the hearty origins associated with a northern country - bread and cheese, roasted and stewed meats, meat and game pies, boiled vegetables and broths, and freshwater and saltwater fish - but has also, thankfully, been influenced by foreign ingredients and cooking styles. Curry was introduced from the Indian subcontinent and adapted to the English palate. French cuisine influenced English recipes throughout the Victorian era. After the Second World War rationing, Elizabeth David's 1950 'A Book of Mediterranean Food' had wide influence and brought Italian cuisine into English homes. Her success encouraged other cookery writers to describe different styles, including Chinese and Thai cuisine. England continues to absorb culinary ideas from all over the world. The United Kingdom is a major consumer but only a very minor producer of wine, with English and Welsh wine sales, combined accounting for just 1% of the domestic market. Due to the cold climate, wine production in the UK has historically been perceived as less than ideal, though the current market is growing. Recent warmer summers have played a role in increasing investment in and sale of wines. Most of the wine produced is of a white and sparkling variety, with most vineyards in existence across Southern England and Wales, where the climate is warmer than that of northern areas.

The County of Kent

The Via Francigena starts in the county of Kent, an area occupied since the Palaeolithic era. The Medway megaliths were built during the Neolithic era, and there is a rich sequence of Bronze Age, Iron Age and Roman era occupation, as indicated by finds and features such as the Ringlemere gold cup and the Roman villas of the Darent valley. The extreme west of the county, as defined today, was occupied by Iron Age tribes known as the Regnenses. East Kent became a kingdom of the Jutes during the 5th century and was known as Cantia from about 730 and as Cent in 835. The early Medieval inhabitants of the county were known as the Cantwara, or Kent people. The modern name of Kent is derived from the Brythonic word Cantus, which means rim or border. Julius Caesar named the area Cantium, or home of the Cantiaci, in 51 BC. During the Medieval and early modern period, Kent played a major role

in several of England's most notable rebellions, including the Peasants' Revolt of 1381, led by Wat Tyler and Wyatt's Rebellion of 1554 against Queen Mary I. Later, in the early 1800s, Kent became associated with smugglers who worked along its coastline. Groups like The Aldington Gang brought spirits, tobacco, and salt to the county and transported goods such as wool across the sea to France. They also created an adventurous mystique that inspired writers like Rudyard Kipling and Mary Waugh. Kent is often called 'The Garden of England' because of its abundance of orchards and hop gardens. The major geographical features of the county are determined by a series of ridges and valleys running east-west across the county, but Kent's location between London and the continent has also led to its being on the front line of several conflicts, including the Battle of Britain during World War II. Between June 1944 and March 1945, over 10,000 V1 flying bombs, known as Doodlebugs, were fired on London from bases in Northern France. Many were destroyed by aircraft, anti-aircraft guns or barrage balloons. Nevertheless, London and Kent were hit by around 2,500 of them and, consequently, given the name Hell Fire Corner.

The Aldington Gang

The first mention of the Aldington Gang was in November 1820, after the men had returned home from the Napoleonic Wars and, finding no other way of making money, started the illegal importation of untaxed contraband from across The Channel.

The Aldington Gang was a band of smugglers that roamed Kent's Romney Marshes and shores. The gang's leaders made The Walnut Tree, a local inn, their headquarters and a place to drop off their contraband. High up on the southern side of the inn is a small window through which the gang would shine a signal light to their partners up on Aldington Knoll when the way was clear for them. In February 1821, the Battle of Brookland took place between the Customs and Excise men and the Aldington Gang. The smugglers had sent 250 men down to the coast between Camber and Dungeness, but the Watch House at Camber saw them, and a fight erupted on Walland Marsh. Their leader at that time was Cephas Quested, who, in the confusion of the Battle, turned to a man close by him, handed him a musket and instructed him to "blow an officer's brains out." Unfortunately for Quested, in the confusion of the fight and being somewhat drunk, the man he had turned to was a Midshipman of the blockade force, who immediately turned the gun on Quested and arrested him. After being sentenced, Quested was taken to Newgate and hanged on 4 July 1821. The success of smuggling gangs was dependent on the goodwill of the local people, and they began to lose this special relationship when they extended their ruthless behaviour beyond that of the publicly acceptable crime of smuggling and instead turned on the rural communities, often robbing private homes. In October 1826, the blockade forces and two Bow Street Runners raided The Bourne Tap, another smuggler's Inn, and captured the leader George Ransley with seven other members of the Gang. Eventually, 19 men stood trial at Maidstone Assizes in January 1827. They were all found guilty of charges that carried the death penalty, but their lawyer managed to get their sentences commuted to transportation.

Canterbury

The Canterbury area has been inhabited since prehistoric times. In the first century AD, the Romans captured the settlement and rebuilt the town with new streets in a grid pattern and a theatre, temple, forum, public baths and later a wall that enclosed an area of 130 acres (53 hectares), with 7 gates. After the Romans left in 410 AD, Durovernum Cantiacorum was abandoned and gradually decayed. Over the next 100 years, an Anglo-Saxon community formed within the city walls, with Jutish (from Jutland) refugees arriving and possibly intermarrying with the locals. The Jutes named the town Cantwaraburh, meaning the Kent people's stronghold. In 597 AD, Pope Gregory the Great sent Augustine to convert King Æthelberht of Kent to Christianity. After the conversion, Canterbury was chosen by Augustine as the centre for an episcopal See (the official seat of a bishop) in Kent, and an abbey and cathedral were built. Thus, the town's new importance led to its revival and trades in pottery, textiles, and leather developed. By 630, gold coins were being struck at the Canterbury Mint. In 672, the Synod of Hertford gave the See of Canterbury authority over the English Church. In 842 and 851, Canterbury suffered great loss of life as a result of Danish raids and during a second wave of attacks in 1011, the cathedral was burnt, and Archbishop Alphege was killed. Later, in 1066, the inhabitants of Canterbury remembered the destruction caused by the Danes and chose not to resist William the Conqueror's invasion. William immediately ordered a wooden motte-and-bailey (a form of castle situated on a raised earthwork and surrounded by a protective fence) to be built by the Roman city wall, and, in the early 12th century, the castle was rebuilt in stone. After the murder of Archbishop Thomas Becket at the cathedral in 1170, Canterbury became one of the most notable towns in Europe, as pilgrims from all parts of Christendom came to visit his shrine. This pilgrimage provided the framework for Geoffrey Chaucer's 14th-century collection of stories, The Canterbury Tales.

Canterbury Cathedral

St Augustine, the first Archbishop of Canterbury, arrived on the coast of Kent as a missionary to England in 597 AD. He was given a church in Canterbury by King Ethelbert, whose Queen, Bertha, was already a Christian. Augustine established his seat within the Roman city walls (cathedra – Latin word for seat) and built the first cathedral there, becoming the first Archbishop of Canterbury. Until the 10th century, the Cathedral community lived as the household of the Archbishop, but it subsequently became a formal community of Benedictine monks, which continued until the monastery was dissolved by King Henry VIII in 1540. Augustine's original building lies beneath the nave floor because the Normans completely rebuilt the Cathedral following a major fire in 1070. There have been many additions to the building over the last 900 years, but some of the windows and their stained glass date from the 12th century. By 1077, Archbishop Lanfranc had rebuilt the cathedral as a Norman church. A staircase and parts of the North Wall - in the area of the North West transept, also called the Martyrdom - remain from that building. Though the Cathedral's role as a monastery ended, its role as a place of prayer continued. The responsibility for the services and upkeep was given to a group of clergy known as the Dean and Chapter. Today, the Cathedral is still governed by the Dean, four Canons, four laypeople, and the Archdeacon of Maidstone. During the Civil War of the 1640s, the Cathedral suffered damage at the hands of the Puritans. Much of the Medieval stained glass was smashed, and horses were stabled in the nave. After the Restoration in 1660, several years were spent repairing the building. In the early 19th Century, the North West tower, dating from Lanfranc's time, was found to be dangerous and was demolished and replaced by a copy of the South West tower, thus giving the symmetrical appearance to the west end of the Cathedral that you see today. During the Second World War, the Precincts were heavily damaged by enemy action, but although the Cathedral's Library was destroyed, the Cathedral itself was not seriously affected.

Thomas Becket

Born in 1120, Beckett was the son of a prosperous London merchant. He was well educated and quickly became an agent to Theobald, Archbishop of Canterbury, who sent him on several missions to Rome. Becket's talents were noticed by Henry II, who made him his chancellor, and the two became close friends. When Theobald died in 1161, Henry made Becket archbishop, and from this point forward, Becket transformed himself from a pleasure-loving courtier into a serious, simply-dressed cleric. However, the friendship between Henry and his archbishop was put under strain when it became clear that Becket would stand up for the church in its disagreements with the king. In 1164, realising the extent of Henry's displeasure, Becket fled to France and remained there until 1170, when Henry offered a compromise that allowed him to return to England. However, the reconciliation did not last long, and it finally ruptured when Becket started to excommunicate his opponents in the church. Hearing reports of Becket's actions, Henry is said to have angrily issued an order that was interpreted by his men as wishing Becket killed. On 29 December 1170, four knights confronted and murdered him in Canterbury Cathedral. Becket was made a saint in 1173, and his Canterbury Cathedral shrine became an important pilgrimage focus.

Chaucer

Geoffrey Chaucer was born in 1340, most likely at his parents' house on Thames Street in London. Chaucer's family was of the bourgeois class and sent their son to St. Paul's Cathedral School, where he probably first became acquainted with the influential writing of Virgil and Ovid. In 1359, the teenage Chaucer went off to fight in the Hundred Years' War in France. Unfortunately, he was captured for ransom, but thanks to his royal connections, King Edward III paid for his release. After this, he joined the Royal

Service, travelling throughout France, Spain and Italy on diplomatic missions until the early to mid-1360s. King Edward III made Chaucer one of his esquires, and from 1370 to 1373, he went abroad again and fulfilled diplomatic missions in Florence and Genoa, helping establish an English port there. During this time, he also familiarised himself with the work of the Italian poets Dante and Petrarch. In 1385, he petitioned for temporary leave to do what he loved most, writing.

The precise dates of many of Chaucer's written works are difficult to pin down with certainty, but his best-known works include the Parliament of Fowls, Troilus and Criseyde - a narrative poem that retells the tragic love story of Troilus and Criseyde in the context of the Trojan War - and The Legend of Good Women. However, The Canterbury Tales is his best-known and most acclaimed work. Initially, Chaucer planned to write four stories a piece for each of his characters. The first two stories would be set as the characters were on their way to Canterbury, and the second two would take place as the character was heading home. In fact, The Canterbury Tales comprises only 24 tales and abruptly ends before its characters even make it to Canterbury. Chaucer died in London on October 25, 1400, at the age of 60. He was buried in Westminster Abbey, and his gravestone became the centre of what is now known as Poet's Corner, a spot where famous British writers, such as Robert Browning and Charles Dickens, were later honoured and interred.

The North Downs Way

On leaving Canterbury, pilgrims join the North Downs Way, which follows the legendary Pilgrims Way, a historic route used by pilgrims travelling to holy shrines. Originally, they would have travelled from Canterbury to Winchester to pray for St

Swithin, buried at the cathedral. Later, this route was used in reverse as pilgrims journeyed from Winchester to Canterbury Cathedral to pray at the shrine of Thomas Becket. From Canterbury, the North Downs Way traces a large part of the route taken by pilgrims travelling to Dover.

Patrixbourne

The Patric family (whose name eventually merged with the Saxon word 'born' to create the present village name) replaced the simple Saxon church in 1170 with a new double-aisled building. The notable similarities between the carvings at Patrixbourne and the celebrated church at nearby Barfreston suggest that the same team of masons worked on both. Above the doorway opening, a tympanum depicts Christ in Majesty, surrounded by a bewildering variety of carved animals, foliage, birds, human figures, and mythical apocalyptic creatures. Among the figures, it is possible to make out a double gryphon, a Green Man, a tortoise, doves, and quite a few others that defy description. Though the chancel was heavily restored in the Victorian period, the windows are all original, including the distinctive wheel window. There are lovely 16th and 17th-century Flemish and Swiss enamelled glass panels in the east windows and the Bifron Chapel.

OF PARTICULAR INTEREST:

Shortly after the village of Patrixbourne, the route passes the entrance to Higham Park, a large neoclassical mansion once home to motor racing driver Count Louis Zborowski, who was perhaps most notable for building and racing cars known as Chitty Bang Bangs. The cars inspired the book, film and stage musical Chitty Chitty Bang Bang. The book's author, Ian Fleming, was just one of the famous visitors to the house throughout its history, along with Wolfgang Amadeus Mozart, Jane Austen and Charles de Gaulle.

Shepherdswell

Shepherdswell is the quintessential English village with quaint cottages, 'olde worlde' pubs and a village green. The village is one of the old coalfield parishes of East Kent and where North Downs Way and Miners Way meet. Also known as Sibertswold, this village is notable for the Shepherdswell memorial (a Celtic Cross) and the Green Man in the church.

The Green Man

The Green Man first appeared in England in the early 12th century and was especially popular in the Gothic architecture of the 13th to 15th centuries. The name 'Green Man' was first used in 1939 by Lady Raglan in an article for the Folklore journal. Before this, the Green Man was known as a foliate head. The Green Man symbolises unity with the natural world and represents the energy of life reborn in Christ. Early Christians adopted the Green Man to symbolize Easter and the Resurrection. The Green Man is also believed to symbolize the cycle of life, death, and rebirth.

Dover

Looming high above the dark waters of the channel, the seven white chalk cliffs of Dover are one of the most recognisable British sights in the world. The Straits of Dover have been Britain's front line and gateway for hundreds of years. Dover controls the English Channel and is known as the Lock and Key of England. Julius Caesar tried to land here during the Roman Invasion of 55 BC, and it was the prime objective of the invasion plans of William the Conqueror, Napoleon and Hitler. In addition to the massive castle, Dover's history as a military and garrison town can be seen in the extensive remains of its Roman and Napoleonic forts and defences from the World Wars when Dover was Britain's front-line town. Today, Dover still relies on the harbour for its prosperity. It is the busiest passenger ferry terminal in the world, the busiest cruise liner terminal in Britain and a major port for freight.

Dover Castle

Dover has always been a chief member of the Cinque Ports' (a historic series of coastal towns in Kent and Sussex), and it was during the reign of Henry II that the castle began to take a recognisable shape. The inner and outer baileys and the great Keep belong to this time. In 1216, a group of rebel barons invited Louis VIII of France to come and take the English crown, but though he had some success breaching the walls, he could not take the castle. The vulnerable north gate, which had been breached in the siege, was converted into an underground forward-defence complex and new gates were built into the outer curtain wall on the western (Fitzwilliam's Gate) and eastern (Constable's Gate) sides. During the siege, the English defenders tunnelled outwards and attacked the French, thus creating the only counter-tunnel in the world. This can still be seen in the Medieval works. By the Tudor age, the defences themselves had been superseded by gunpowder, and, during the English Civil War, the castle was held for the king but then taken by a parliamentarian trick without a shot being fired. Massive rebuilding occurred at the end of the 18th century and during the Napoleonic Wars. With Dover becoming a garrison town, there was a need for barracks and storerooms for the additional troops and their equipment, so instead, the Royal Engineers created a complex of tunnels about 15 metres below the cliff top. The first troops were accommodated in 1803, and at the height of the Napoleonic Wars, the tunnels housed more than 2000 men. To date, they are the only underground barracks ever built in Britain. At the end of the Napoleonic Wars, the tunnels were partly converted and used by the Coast Blockade Service to combat smuggling. However, this was a short-term endeavour, and in 1826, the headquarters were moved closer to shore. The tunnels remained abandoned for over a century until World War II when they were first converted into an air-raid shelter and later into a military command centre and underground hospital. In May 1940, Admiral Sir Bertram Ramsay directed the evacuation of French and British soldiers from Dunkirk (codenamed Operation Dynamo) from his headquarters in the cliff tunnels. Later, the tunnels were to be used as a shelter for the Regional Seats of Government in the event of a nuclear attack, but this plan was abandoned when it was found that the chalk of the cliffs would not provide significant protection from radiation, and because of the inconvenient form of the tunnels and their generally poor condition. In November 2000, a statue of Admiral Sir Bertram Ramsay was erected outside the tunnels in honour of his work on the Dunkirk evacuation and protection of Dover.

John Bunyan

Before leaving British shores, mention has to be made of John Bunyan, Britain's famed author of 'The Pilgrim's Progress.' John Bunyan was born near Bedford in 1628. His father was a brazier or tinker, and John was brought up to follow his father's trade. When he was sixteen, Bunyan lost his mother and two sisters, who died within months of each other. In 1649, Bunyan married Mary, an orphan, and described their life as being "as poor as poor might be". In his autobiographical book, Grace Abounding, Bunyan describes himself as having led an abandoned life in his youth and as having been morally reprehensible, though there appears to be no evidence that he was outwardly worse than his neighbours - examples of sins to which he confesses are profanity, dancing and bell-ringing. The increasing awareness of his apparently un-Biblical life led him to be tortured by the fear that he was guilty of what he described as the "unpardonable sin". In 1655, after moving his family to Bedford, both Bunyan's wife and his mentor, John Gifford, died. Bunyan was utterly grief-stricken, and his health declined, but despite this, he went on to become a deacon of St. Paul's Church, Bedford and began preaching with marked success. But, as his popularity and notoriety grew, Bunyan increasingly became a target for slander and libel. He was accused of being a witch, a Jesuit, and a highwayman and was said to have mistresses and multiple wives. In 1658, aged 30, he

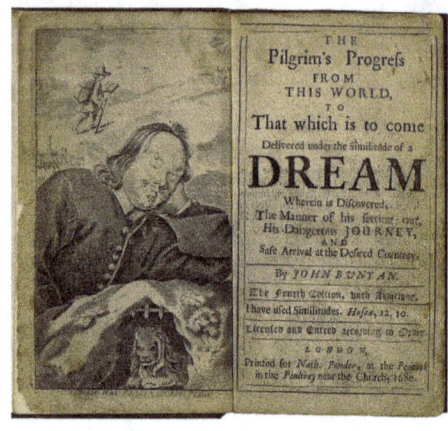
was arrested for preaching at Eaton Socon and, in 1658, was indicted for preaching without a license. Finally, in November 1660, he was taken to Silver Street, Bedford jail. Initially, he was confined for three months, but when he refused to conform or stop preaching, his confinement was extended for nearly twelve years. During this time, he conceived his allegorical novel, The Pilgrim's Progress. In 1666, he was briefly released for a few weeks before he was arrested again for preaching and sent back to Bedford jail for another six years. During this time, he preached to an imprisoned congregation of about sixty parishioners. Bunyan was released in January 1672 (when Charles II issued the Declaration of Religious Indulgence) and became pastor of St. Paul's Church in the same month. In addition, he established over thirty new congregations and was given the affectionate title of Bishop Bunyan by his parishioners. In March 1675, he was again imprisoned for preaching. Still, ironically, it was the Quakers who helped secure his release. As a result of his popularity, he was not arrested again. In 1688, he served as chaplain to Sir John Shorter, the Lord Mayor of London, but as he was riding to London from Reading to resolve a disagreement, he caught a cold, developed a fever

and died at the house of his friend, John Strudwick. He was buried in the cemetery at Bunhill Fields in London, and many Puritans (for whom worship of tombs or relics is considered most sinful) made it their dying wish that their coffins be placed as close to Bunyan's as possible. In 1862, a recumbent statue was created to adorn his grave. He lies among other historical nonconformists, such as George Fox, William Blake, and Daniel Defoe.

France

France has the only two things towards which we drift as we grow older - intelligence and manners.

F. Scott Fitzgerald

Often referred to as L'Hexagone because of the geometric shape of its territory, France is bordered by Belgium, Luxembourg, Germany, Switzerland, Italy, and Monaco, with Spain and Andorra to the south. France has been a major power for several centuries with strong economic, cultural, military and political influence in Europe and abroad. France was also a founding member state of the European Union and the largest one in the area. The name France comes from Latin Francia, meaning land of the Franks or country of the Franks. Today, the borders of modern France

are approximately the same as those of ancient Gaul, which was conquered by Rome under Julius Caesar in the 1st century BC. The Gauls eventually adopted the Roman language (Latin) and culture. Christianity first appeared in the 2nd and 3rd centuries AD and became so firmly established by the 4th and 5th centuries that St. Jerome wrote that Gaul was the only region "free from heresy". The monarchical rule reached its height during the 17th century and the reign of Louis XIV. At this time, France had the largest population in Europe and had tremendous influence on European politics, economy, and culture. The French Revolution challenged the monarchy, though it did not fall immediately after the storming of the Bastille on 14 July 1789, but endured until the creation of the First Republic in September 1792. After a series of short-lived governmental schemes, Napoleon Bonaparte seized control of the Republic in 1799, making himself First Consul and later Emperor. Today, the French Republic is a unitary semi-presidential republic. The constitution of the Fifth Republic was approved by referendum on 28 September 1958 and greatly strengthened the executive's authority concerning parliament. France is ranked as the first tourist destination in the world because it has so much to offer: high mountain plateaus, lush farmland, traditional villages, chic boulevards, Medieval architecture ranging from small Romanesque churches to huge Gothic cathedrals and, of course, the charm of rural living – though this is in fact changing. Whereas in 1945, one person in three worked on the land, today it is only one in sixteen. Culture, on the other hand, is still taken very seriously. Writers, artists and intellectuals are highly esteemed, and the state finances a large network of provincial theatres. French cooking is also world-renowned. Even the most basic traditional meal consists of at least 3 courses. Finally, and unforgettably, France has its wines, an expertise that has continued to develop the reputation of fine wines such as Bourdeaux, Burgundy, the Rhône and Champagne, so that they have become role models the world over.

The department of Pas-de Calais

Your first step off the ferry will be in the Department of Pas-de-Calais. Since prehistoric times, the Pas-de-Calais region was inhabited by the Celtic Belgae, the Romans, the Germanic Franks, and the Alemanni. During the 4th and 5th centuries, the Roman practice of co-opting Germanic tribes to provide military and defence services along the route from Boulogne-sur-Mer to Cologne created a Germanic-Romance linguistic border in the region that persisted until the 8th century.

Saxon colonization into the region from the 5th to the 8th centuries likely extended the linguistic border somewhat south and west so that by the 9th century, most inhabitants north of the line between Béthune and Berck spoke a dialect of Middle Dutch, while the inhabitants to the south spoke Picard, a variety of Romance dialects. Some of the costliest battles of World War I were fought in the region, and it was also the target of Operation Fortitude during World War II, which was an Allied plan to deceive the Germans that the invasion of Europe at D-Day was to occur here, rather than in Normandy. Pas-de-Calais shares a nominal border with the English county of Kent halfway through the Channel Tunnel. Its principal coastal towns are Calais, Boulogne-sur-Mer and Étaples. As for the cuisine, the most renowned specialities are andouillette de Cambrai (a coarse-grained sausage made with pork intestines), chicory gratin, anguille au vert à la Flamande (eel in a green herb sauce). For the sweet tooth, the specialities include gâteau Carpeaux (chestnut cake), la gaufre à la chicorée (chicory waffle), tuiles d'Arras (thin cookies), and bêtises de Cambrai, a boiled sweet made in the town of the same name.

Calais

The closest French town to England, Calais overlooks the Straits of Dover, the narrowest point in the English Channel, which is only 34 kilometres wide at this point. On a clear day, the white cliffs of Dover can easily be seen from Calais. The old part of the town, Calais-Nord, is situated on an artificial island surrounded by canals and harbours. The modern part, St-Pierre, lies to the south and southeast. Virtually the entire town was destroyed by heavy bombardments during World War II, so little in Calais pre-dates it, and for most visitors, it is simply a place to pass through on their way to other destinations. The town centre is dominated by its distinctive city hall, built in the Flemish Renaissance style, with the statue Les Bourgeois de Calais, by Auguste Rodin, directly in front. The German wartime military headquarters, situated near the train station in a small park, is now open to the public as a war museum. From Calais, the route leads along the Cote d'Opale, where long sandy beaches are exposed by huge tidal flows against high chalk cliffs. This section skirts the Cap Blanc-Nez and offers spectacular views over the sea and surrounding countryside. On the way, look out for the statue in memory of Louis Blériot, the celebrated aViator.

Louis Blériot

Louis Blériot was born in Cambrai, France, on 1 July 1872. While studying engineering in Paris, he developed an interest in aviation. Since the early 19th century, Frenchmen such as Jean Pierre François Blanchard and Jacob Degen had been building ornithopters, which are machines that fly by flapping their wings. In 1900, Blériot built his own ornithopter, but like Blanchard and Degen, he failed to get it off the ground. In 1903, Blériot joined another aircraft designer, Gabriel Voisin, to form the Blériot-Voison Company. The company built a floatplane glider, which flew in 1905. The following year, Blériot left Voison and started his own company, where he built a monoplane with a tractor propeller. Alfred Harmsworth, the owner of the Daily Mail newspaper, was a great supporter of flying and, in October 1908, offered a prize of £1,000 for the first airman to cross the English Channel from Calais to Dover. Blériot decided he would make an attempt and began work on a new plane, the Blériot XI. On 25 July 1909, Blériot took off from Les Baraques, near Calais, at 4.41am. After covering a distance of almost 24 kilometres, he arrived at Northfall Meadow, near Dover, at 5.17 am. One man wrote, "England's isolation has ended once and for all."

Sangatte

Like many place names in French Flanders, Sangatte is of Flemish (Dutch) origin, and Zandgat means gap in the sand. Look out for the statue of Hubert Latham overlooking the sea - another pioneering cross-channel pilot, but whose earlier attempt had failed.

Wissant

Located at the eastern end of an ancient lagoon, Wissant, formerly a part of the parish of Sombre, has long been a fishing village (the last fishing village in France to use a traditional method of fishing off a wooden boat called a flobart) and was once the major port for access to England. Many historians believe Julias Caesar embarked from here for his conquest of England in 55 BC. this made it an important Channel port long before Calais was developed by the English (1347 – 1558).

Pilgrims flocking to or from England used to file through Wissant, and the plaque shown on a church wall reminds everyone of Thomas Becket's last return journey to England, where he met his death 28 days later. At the end of the 19th century, the coastal dunes of Wissant began to cover the seaside villas, but in the 20th century, an entrepreneur, Mr Létendart from Calais, extracted sand and gravel from the dunes to the west of Wissant and resolved the problem. The subsequent excavations now form lakes and a nature reserve

Sombre LXXX Sumeran

Jean-Pierre Blanchard

Jean-Pierre Blanchard was a French inventor and the pioneer of gas balloon flight. Notable for his successful hydrogen balloon flight in Paris on 2 March 1784, Blanchard later moved to London and undertook flights with varying propulsion mechanisms. His historic

achievement came on 7 January 1785, when he crossed the English Channel from Dover Castle to Guînes in about 2½ hours, receiving acclaim from Louis XVI and earning a substantial pension.

Following the invention of the modern parachute in 1783 by Sébastien Lenormand in France, Jean-Pierre Blanchard demonstrated it as a means of jumping safely from a balloon. While Blanchard's first parachute demonstrations were conducted with a dog as the passenger, he later had the opportunity to try it himself when his hydrogen balloon ruptured, and he used a parachute to escape. Subsequent development of the parachute focused on making it more compact. While the early parachutes were made of linen stretched over a wooden frame, in the late 1790s, Blanchard began making parachutes from folded silk, taking advantage of silk's strength and lightweight. Blanchard made his first successful balloon flight in Paris on 2 March 1784, in a hydrogen gas balloon launched from the Champ de Mars, but his flight nearly ended in disaster when one spectator (Dupont de Chambon, a contemporary of Napoleon at the École militaire de Brienne) slashed at the balloon's mooring ropes and oars with his sword after being refused a place on board. Blanchard intended to proceed northeast to La Villette, but the balloon was pushed by the wind across the Seine to  Billancourt and back again, until he eventually landed in the rue de Sèvres. These early balloon flights triggered a phase of public balloonomania, with all kinds of objects decorated with images of balloons and 'clothing au ballon' was produced with exaggerated puffed sleeves and rounded skirts. Hair was coiffed 'à la montgolfier' or à la Blanchard'.

Blanchard moved to London in August 1784, where he took part in a flight on 16 October 1784 with John Sheldon, just a few weeks after the first flight in Britain (and the first outside France), when Italian Vincenzo Lunardi flew from Moorfields to Ware on 15 September 1784. Blanchard's propulsion mechanisms – flapping wings and a windmill – proved ineffective, but the balloon flew some 115 km from Lewis Lochée's military academy in Little Chelsea, landed in Sunbury and then took off again to end in Romsey. Blanchard took a second flight on 30 November 1784, taking off with an American, Dr John Jeffries, from the Rhedarium behind Green Street Mayfair, London, to Ingress in Kent.

In 1793, he conducted the first balloon flight in the Americas, when he launched his balloon from the prison yard of Walnut Street Jail in Philadelphia, Pennsylvania and landed in Deptford, Gloucester County, New Jersey. One of the flight's witnesses that day was President George Washington, and the future presidents John Adams, Thomas Jefferson, James Madison, and James Monroe were also present.

On 20 February 1808 Blanchard had a heart attack while in his balloon at The Hague. He fell from the balloon and died roughly a year later due to severe injuries. His widow, Marie Madeleine-Sophie Armant (better known as Sophie Blanchard), continued to support herself with ballooning demonstrations until doing so also killed her.

Guînes   LXXVIII Gisne

Guînes is the first town identified by Sigeric hat you will pass through.   It is located on the border of the two territories of the Boulonnais and Calaisis, at the edge of the now-drained marshes, which extend from there to the coast. The Guînes canal connects with Calais. Guînes is notable as the site of one of the earliest and, perhaps, most famous Summit Meetings, though it would not have been recognised as such at the time, known as the the Field of the Cloth of Gold. And finally Guînes is notable because On 7 January 1785, Jean-Pierre Blanchard, a French pioneer in hydrogen-balloon flight, completed the first crossing of the English Channel and landed in the woods south of Guînes where a memorial column stands today.

Field of the Cloth of Gold

After seeing his kingdom divided by the French royal family and royal marriages, which latterly put Flanders under Spanish rule, François I, the new King of France, feared being surrounded on both sides by Spain and so started to consider an alliance with England. Though a tiny country compared with France, England (under Henry VII and Henry VIII) had built up Europe's most modern navy, and as a growing sea power, it was potentially a good ally for France against Spain. With this in mind, Francis persuaded Henry VIII to attend a meeting between the two monarchs at a location within travelling distance of Calais. Henry and Francis were personal and political rivals, and each king prided himself on the magnificence of his court. Huge pavilions were erected to serve as halls and chapels, and great silken tents were decorated with gold gems and cloth. This ostentatious display of wealth and power earned the meeting place the sobriquet 'The Field of the Cloth of Gold.' The event lasted for three weeks (7-24 June - 7 1520), during which time each court strove to outdo the other in offering splendid entertainment and making grandiose gestures. Feasts and jousts were held, including a tilt between Henry and Francis. Balls, masques, fireworks and military sports were just some of the activities on offer, incurring enormous expenses and putting tremendous strain on the finances of each country. Nevertheless, the results of the meeting were negligible. Though Henry and Francis agreed in principle to an alliance, over the next several years, the alliances were broken and reformed in an ever-shifting attempt to gain ascendancy in Europe, with no one gaining any permanent advantage.

Wisques

This village is deceptive. Despite being tiny, it is home to two significant religious communities that belong to the order of Saint Benedict, Notre Dame (convent) and Saint Paul (monastery).

Saint Paul's Abbey was built at the end of the 15th century by the Saint-Aldegonde family but has undergone many changes over the centuries. First housed in the Petit Château, a fine 18th-century mansion opposite the present-day cemetery, the monks later moved to the Grand Château, which they still occupy today. The most noteworthy parts of the buildings are the bell tower, the keep (built at the end of the Middle Ages), and parts renovated by Dom Bellot (Parisian, born into a family of architects and later a monk). An additional bell tower was built in 1945 to house Bertine, the only bell from the old Saint-Bertin's abbey to withstand the ravages of the French Revolution. Dating from 1470, it weighs 7.5 tons and is a listed monument. The tower of the present-day chapel was built in 1957, and the abbey was further extended in 1968, when the reception building was fully renovated and redecorated, with Retreat accommodation provided in a modern building of the two abbeys.

Notre Dame, founded in 1889 by the nuns of Saint Cécile of Solesmes, was originally lodged in part of the Grand Château but relocated when the Abbey of Notre Dame was built in 1891. The building layout was created by Lille architect Paul Vilain, who was considered to be the most eminent representative of the neo-gothic school in the north of France.

Today, the Community of the Abbey of Notre Dame at Wisques is made up of about twenty sisters of all ages, happy to live together fraternally according to the Rule of St Benedict.

Paul Vilain

After studying at the Saint-Luc arts schools in Lille and then in Ghent, Paul Vilain graduated in architecture in 1885. He then directed the construction of the Ladies of the Saint-Sacrement convent in Rome before settling in Lille in 1887, where a firm bearing his name was founded at 24, rue Catel-Béghin. A fervent Catholic, he was chosen by the board of directors of Treille to succeed Charles Leroy as director of the construction site of the Notre-Dame-de-la-Treille cathedral in Lille in

1889. He was then approved to work on communes, hospices, and public establishments in the Nord department in 1897. In 1920, he took the Swiss architect Charles-Paul Serex into his agency, who became his partner in 1930. During his first design period, Paul Vilain combined monumental neo-Gothic and functionalism stemming from the teaching of Louis Cloquet. After the First World War, it evolved towards more modern formulas with the use of concrete which took it towards an Art Deco style.

Licques

Today, the small town of Licques is famous for the turkeys it rears in time for Christmas every year. The birds are paraded through the streets during its Fête de la Dinde - preceded by the Confrerie de Licques (the town's VIPs) - before being slaughtered and stuffed with chestnuts on Christmas day. The hen of India was introduced to Licques by the local monks and raised on an excellent free-range diet of roots, seeds, and worms living in the damp valley soils. Sales to the Licques villagers started when the birds began to reproduce faster than they could be eaten, and before long, the local farmers were getting in on the act and breeding their own stock. Consequently, the entire region became famous for its tender and tasty meat, which is now sold throughout the year.

Esquerdes

The village's name first appeared as Squerda in 857, later known as Ekarde, and finally as Esquerdes. The settlement was on the Roman road from Thérouanne to Sangatte on the coast. An archaeological survey of 1984 revealed traces of the Neolithic period (flint and carved bone) at two sites known as Les Tripoux and Le Paradis. The story of Esquerdes is linked to the development of two major industries, paper and gunpowder making, which developed from the time of Louis XIV until the 19th century and led to a large population growth. In 1790, the town was large enough, with its 500 inhabitants, to be appointed chief town of the canton - two hundred years later, this figure has more than tripled.

OF PARTICULAR INTEREST:

- The private Crèvecoeur farm, near the river, has many buildings dating from the 15th century. These belonged to John de Trémoillepuis and his son, Philippe de Crèvecoeur, who served under Charles the Bold, Duke of Burgundy and Kings Louis XI and Charles VII.

Thérouanne LXXVII Teranburh

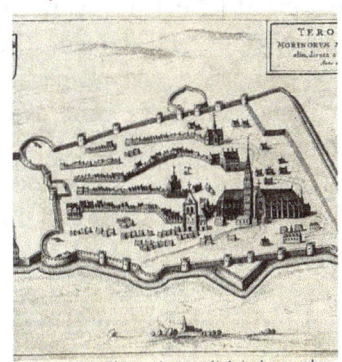

The origin of the name has several theories. According to the historian Malbracq, it got its name from its founder Lucius Tauruannus. Others say it is derived from Terra avanae, The land of Oats. Nestling in the Lys valley, Thérouanne used to be the capital of Morini before it became the seat of one of the wealthiest bishoprics in the North of France and a favourite stopping place for pilgrims following the Via Francigena. While at war with François I, Charles V ordered that the town be destroyed, along with all of its civic and religious buildings.

OF PARTICULAR INTEREST

- The cathedral of Thérouanne, whose construction was begun in the 12th century, is one of the finest Gothic cathedrals in the North of France.
- The Archaeological site where the ruins of the foundations of the old cathedral can be seen.
- The Archeology Museum houses three exhibition rooms presenting Thérouanne in the Gallo-Roman period, Thérouanne over the ages and Medieval objects found at the former site of the cathedral. In addition, you can see an authentic parchment bearing the seal of Charles V, dated 11 July 1553, containing the order to demolish the town.
- The Chapel of Nielles les Thérouanne, the last vestige of the ancient city.

The Siege of Thérouanne

Henry VIII had joined the Holy League with Venice and Spain to defend the Papacy from its enemies and France with military force. In May 1513, English soldiers began to arrive in Calais to join an army commanded by George Talbot, Earl of Shrewsbury. Henry VIII arrived in person at Calais on 30 June 1513, with the main grouping of 11,000 men. The army, provided by Cardinal Thomas Wolsey, comprised several martial forces, including cavalry, artillery, infantry, and longbows, and used hardened steel arrows designed to penetrate armour more effectively. Thérouanne fell to the English on August 22nd, and the day was soon called the Battle of the Spurs (La Journée d'Esperons) because of the hasty departure of the French horses from the battlefield. The town's walls were pushed into the deep defensive ditches, and its houses burned. When Pope Leo X was told of the English victories, his congratulations were conveyed to Cardinal Wolsey. Emporer Maximilian also commissioned woodcut images of his meeting with Henry, which included a scene of the mounted rulers joining hands in the Triumphal Arch.

Saint Audomar

Better known as Saint-Omer, he was a Burgundy-born bishop of Thérouanne, after whom nearby Saint-Omer was named. He was born into a distinguished family in Switzerland, but after the death of his mother, he entered (with his father) the abbey of Luxeuil in the Diocese of Besançon. Under the direction of Eustachius, Omer studied the Scriptures and displayed remarkable proficiency. When King Dagobert requested the appointment of a bishop for the important city of Terouenne, the capital of the ancient territory of the Morini in Neustria, Audomar was appointed

and consecrated in 637. Though the Morini had received Christianity from Saint Fuscian, Saint Victoricus, and later Antmund and Adelbert, nearly every vestige had disappeared. In 654, he founded the Abbey of Saint Peter (now Saint Bertin's) in Sithiu, soon to equal if not surpass the old monastery of Luxeuil for the number of learned and zealous men educated there. Several years later, he erected the Church of Our Lady of Sithiu with a small monastery adjoining it. The exact date of his death is unknown, but he is believed to have died in 670 and probably laid to rest in the church of Our Lady, which is now the Cathédrale Notre-Dame de Saint-Omer.

Liettres

It is worth stopping in Liettres to see Chateau Liettres, built in 1479 by Sir Simon de Luxembourg, provost of the church of Saint-Omer. Raised on an artificial embankment in the marshy valley of the Laquette, which fed the moats, the castle was then composed of four main buildings, forming approximately a square flanked by large cylindrical towers. After being repaired after the fire of 1479, the fortress was once again burned in 1542 by the troops of the Duke of Vandôme. In its current state, the castle still has two powerful circular towers, which give it the characteristic appearance of a Medieval fortress.

Amettes

Best known as the birthplace of Saint Benedict Joseph Labre (1748-1783), Amettes is a typical farming village for the region. The church of St. Sulpice, dating from the 16th century, is also typical of its kind.

Joseph Labre

A French mendicant and, latterly, a Roman Catholic saint, Joseph Labre was born in Amettes, the eldest of fifteen children of a prosperous shopkeeper. From a very early age, Labre was noted for performing public acts of penance for his sins, even minor ones. At the age of sixteen, he attempted to join the Trappists, Carthusians and Cistercians, but each order rejected him as unsuitable for communal life. The abbots of these orders suspected some form of mental illness, which would make Labre unable to fulfil the vow of obedience necessary for any cloistered religious life. He took this as a sign that it was God's will that he should abandon his country and his parents to lead "A life most painful, most penitential, not in a wilderness nor in a cloister, but in the midst of the world,

devoutly visiting as a pilgrim the famous places of Christian devotion." Saint Benedict first travelled to Rome on foot, subsisting on what he could receive by begging. He then travelled to most of the major shrines of Europe, often multiple times. He visited Loreto, Assisi, Naples and Bari in Italy, Einsiedeln in Switzerland, Paray-le-Monial in France and Compostela in Spain. During these trips, he would always travel on foot, sleep in the open or in the corner of a room, and wear his clothes muddy and ragged. He lived on what little he was given and often shared the little he did receive with others. He is reported to have talked rarely, prayed often and quietly accepted the abuse he received, thus conforming to the role of the mendicant, the Fool-for-Christ, found more often in the Eastern Church. In the last years of his life (his 30s), he lived in the walls of the ruins of the Colosseum in Rome. In his final weeks, he collapsed in church and, despite his protestations, was taken into a house out of charity. He died of malnutrition during Holy Week in 1783. The 15th-century Saint-Sulpice church in the centre of Amettes holds the saint's kneecaps and the straw mattress he is said to have died on. On the walls, fourteen scenes retrace the path of the saint's life and in the choir, contemporary stained-glass windows (fitted in 1975) depict the most important stages. From Amettes, the Via Francigena follows a road first created by the Romans, though it is now known as Chaussée Brunehaut, which links Therouanne to Arras.

Chaussée Brunehaut

Brunehaut, or Brunhilde, was raised as an Arian Christian but converted to Roman Catholicism after marrying Sigebert. From here, she took a keen personal interest in the bishoprics and monasteries within her dominion and incidentally commissioned the building of several churches and the abbey of St. Vincent in Laon (580). Unfortunately, the rest of her history is less positive, and it appears she became embroiled in some unsavoury assassinations. Ultimately, this behaviour led to her own death when according to the Liber Historiae Francorum: "The army of Franks and Burgundians joined into one, agreeing all together that death would be most fitting for the very wicked Brunhilda. King Clotaire ordered that she be lifted on to a camel and led through the entire army. Then she was tied to the feet of wild horses and torn apart limb from limb. Finally, she died. Her final grave was the fire. Her bones were burnt."

Bruay la Buissière   LXXVI Bruwaei

The name of this town has undergone many changes before becoming what it is today. The source is in the old French word 'buissy', meaning a wooden box. From here, it evolved to become Bruxeria, then to Boesère, Bouchière, Buissière, and then, finally, in 1725, became Bruay La Buissière. Some Roman archaeological discoveries have been made in the area and can be seen in the town - principally a figurine of Venus, along with evidence of clay-making and a furnace for the firing of clay pots. Bruay la Buissèrie and the surrounding area bear the scars of two world wars. In the First World War, British pilots Watt (27) and Howlett (26) lost their lives during an aerial battle with the infamous Red Baron. They were buried near the town alongside their French and Canadian allies. During the Second World War, several Bruaysiennes became members of the resistance and were later recognised for their bravery. Like the rest of France, the people struggled with rationing and the oppression of living in an occupied country. Liberation came on 4 September 1944, with the arrival of the Canadians, but not before thirty-three people had died. In 1720, coal was discovered near Bruay la Buissèrie, with eight shafts operating until 1976. During the 1920s, an increase in the population of Bruay la Buissèrie was needed to meet the labour needs of the mines, and the result was that a large Polish immigrant community was established, and it still remains today. Houses had to be rapidly built to accommodate the new residents, and from 1938 to 1968, the city grew from 5,803 houses to 9,559. Marles les Mines is well worth taking a detour to visit.

Courrières mine disaster

As you leave Bruay, look out for a plaque commemorating Europe's worst mining accident, which caused the death of 1,099 miners, including many children, when a dust explosion devastated a mine between Méricourt, Sallaumines, Billy-Montigny, and Noyelles-sous-Lens. A large explosion was heard shortly after 06:30 on Saturday, 10 March 1906 and an elevator cage was blasted up to the surface, damaging pit-head workings. About 600 miners were able to reach the surface during the hours immediately after the explosion, but many were severely burned and/or suffered the effects of mine gases. A group of thirteen survivors, known later as the escapés, was found by rescuers on 30 March, twenty days after the explosion. They had survived first by eating the food which the victims had taken underground for their lunch and later by slaughtering one of the mine horses. The two eldest (39 and 40 years old) were awarded the Légion d'honneur, and the other eleven (including three younger than eighteen) received the Médaille d'or du courage. A final survivor was found on 4 April.

Ablain-Saint-Nazaire

This little farming village is not immediately noteworthy, but like so many places in this area, it bears the scars of the last two World Wars. At the start of World War I, the Battle of Lorette lasted from October 1914 to October 1915, resulting in high casualties on both sides: 100,000 killed and as many wounded. A French national cemetery was built on thirteen hectares nearby and comprises 20,000 graves, laid out irrespective of rank or military training. In eight ossuaries around the base of the lantern tower hold the remains of 22,970 unidentified soldiers. A portion of the cemetery has also been reserved for Muslim soldiers. Unusually for a community of this size, Ablain-Saint-Naziare has two churches. In the centre of the village, you will find a church dating from the inter-war period, and to the east, a 16th-century church ruined but still a masterpiece of flamboyant Gothic designed by the architect Jacques Le Caron. This church was built at the behest of local lord Charles de Bourbon-Carency in recognition of the part Saint Nazarius played in healing his sick daughter.

Mont-Saint-Eloi Abbey Towers

If you take the alternative route, you will see the Mont-Saint-Eloi towers on

a hill overlooking Arras. They are the remains of two towers which bear testament to the once-powerful Mont-Saint-Eloi Abbey and the savage fighting in the area during the Great War. According to legend, the abbey was established in the 7th century by Saint Vindicianus, a disciple of Saint Eligius (Saint Eloi in French), and by the Middle Ages, it had become a powerful religious centre. Unfortunately, its walls were pillaged for their stone during the Revolution, and all that survived were the twin towers of white limestone that you will see today. In 1915, heavy shelling truncated the towers, reducing their height from 53 to 44 metres. In 1921, they were finally listed on France's register of ancient monuments and have since undergone much-needed work to consolidate their structure.

Arras   LXXV Atherats

Arras - a tapestry, especially one with complex stitches that is hung as a decoration.

Flemish culture still holds sway along the border with Belgium, so now you will find yourself meandering through an unfamiliar France of windmills and canals, where the local taste is for beer, savoury stews and festivals with gallivanting giants. Arras is one of northern France's most architecturally striking towns, the cobblestoned squares of its old centre surrounded by ornate Baroque townhouses that hark back to its Flemish past. Reconstruction after the war was meticulous, and the townhouses lining the grand arcaded Flemish and Dutch-style squares in the central Grand'Place and the smaller Place des Héros preserve the historic character perfectly. Arras was on the border between France and the Low Countries for centuries and frequently changed hands before firmly becoming French. In the late 17th century, Vauban upgraded the fortifications, helping to keep it in French hands. The town was closely linked to the trade of Flanders and later became an important centre for sugar beet farming and processing, as well as a prosperous market centre. In the 14th and 15th centuries, Arras was a thriving textile town, specialising in fine wool tapestries that decorated palaces and castles all over Europe. Few of these tapestries survived the French Revolution when hundreds were burnt to recover the gold thread often woven into them. Nevertheless, the term arras is still used to refer to a rich tapestry, no matter where it was woven. A handful of the famous Medieval Arras tapestries were protected and survived the conflict, including The Annunciation, now on display in the Metropolitan Museum of Art, New York. The Union of Utrecht (the Dutch name for Arras) was signed here in January 1579 by the Catholic principalities of the Low Countries, which remained loyal to King Phillip II of Habsburg, provoking the declaration of the Union of Utrecht in the same month. During the First World War, Arras was near the front, and the long series of battles fought nearby are known as the Battle of Arras. A series of Medieval tunnels beneath the city, unknown to the Germans, became a decisive factor in the British forces holding of Arras (guided tours available). Even so, the city was heavily damaged and had to be rebuilt after the war. In World War II, 240 suspected French Resistance members were executed in the Arras citadel. Today, Arras has thoroughly absorbed its historical past as a pilgrim thoroughfare, and as you walk, you can look down and see signs on the pavement for both the Via Francigena and St James Way.

OF PARTICULAR INTEREST:

- The Belfry Tower, a Unesco World Heritage Site, offers a splendid view over Arras and the surrounding countryside. Access to the first ring of the bell tower is Via a lift or 40+ steps.

- The underground Jardin des Boves is only open in spring but is ten metres or so beneath the paving stones of Arras.

- Saint-Vaast Abbey and the Cathedral form France's largest 18th-century religious architectural grouping. Founded in the 7th century, the construction of the Abbey marked the birth of the Medieval town. The huge scale of the building today accurately reflects its economic and spiritual role in the town's artistic and cultural development. The Cathedral houses sculptures of saints from the Pantheon and the Aubusson tapestry, among other things.

- The Nemetacum Site, founded 2,000 years ago by the Romans, is part of the ancient town of Nemetacum and is now open to view. The archaeological remains are testimony to the daily life of people living in the capital of the Atrebates.

Vauban

Sébastien Le Prestre de Vauban (15 May 1633 - 30 March 1707) was from a family of modest means, but when, in 1651, he became a cadet in the regiment of Louis II de Bourbon, his talents were soon revealed. Considered an expert in his field, rivalled only by his Dutch contemporary Menno van Coehoorn, his design principles served as the dominant fortification model for nearly 100 years, while his offensive tactics remained in use until the early 20th century. Vauban introduced the innovative use of siege artillery and founded the Corps Royal des Ingénieurs Militaires. Vauban worked on many of France's major ports and harbours, as well as civilian infrastructure projects like the Canal de la Bruche, and published on engineering design, strategy, and training. Shortly before his death, in 1707, he produced an economic tract entitled La Dîme Royale, which was later destroyed by Royal decree because it contained radical proposals for a more even distribution of the tax burden. Using statistics to support his arguments makes the work a precursor of modern economics. His application of rational and scientific methods to problem-solving, whether engineering or social, anticipated an approach that became common in the Age of Enlightenment. Finally, one of the most significant and enduring aspects of Vauban's legacy was his view of France as a geographical and economic entity; as a result, the boundaries established in the north and east have changed very little in the four centuries since.

Bapaume

This small country town is on a crossing point between Artois and the plains of Flanders on the one hand and the valley of the Somme and the Paris basin on the other - a position that made it the focal point for wars throughout its history. In 1335, Bapaume was fortified outside the castle walls, but unfortunately, the fortifications were ineffective, and the city was repeatedly taken. In 1540, Charles Quint ordered a fortified palace with thick walls and bastions, including defensive systems such as tunnels and galleries. These fortifications were later reinforced by Vauban.

By the 19th century, Bapaume was no longer considered a fortified town. The walls and bastions were blown up, and the moats were filled in. Only the tower and part of the bastion of Dauphin are still visible. Work has been done recently to restore and make accessible the underground galleries used as shelters during both world wars.

The department of The Somme

The Somme department is named after the Somme River, and Amiens is its capital. The Bay of Somme is the biggest estuary in the north of France, extending over 70 kilometres between the headland of Hourdel and Saint Quentin en Tourmont. Le Crotoy, on the Somme's coastline, has played host to several famous names over the centuries, including Joan of Arc (who was imprisoned here), Jacques-Francois Conseil (first physician of the French colony of Guyana) and more recently, Jules Verne (French author who helped pioneer the science fiction genre). Slightly further down the coast, in St-Valery-sur-Somme, William the Conqueror set off for England in 1066. The many cemeteries that cover the Somme region serve as poignant reminders of the mass slaughter that took place on the Western Front in World War 1 (which ended with the Armistice on November 11, 1918). Between July 1 and November 21, 1916, the Allied forces lost more than 600,000 men and the Germans at least 465,000. The Battle of the Somme, a series of campaigns conducted by British and French armies against fortified positions held by the Germans, relieved the hard-pressed French at Verdun, but the Allies only managed to advance sixteen kilometres. One German officer, General D. Swaha, famously described the campaign as "the muddy grave of the German field army." By the end of the battle, the British had learned many lessons in modern warfare, while the Germans had suffered irreplaceable losses. British historian Sir James Edmonds stated, "It is not too much to claim that the foundations of the final victory on the Western Front were laid by the Somme offensive of 1916."

Joan of Arc

To understand Joan of Arc, we must see her in the context of the time. The Hundred Years' War began in 1337 as an inheritance dispute over the French throne, interspersed with occasional periods of relative peace. Nearly all the fighting had taken place in France, and the English army's use of chevauchée (scorched earth) tactics had devastated the economy.

The French population had not regained its former size since the Black Death of the mid-14th century, and its merchants were isolated from foreign markets. Charles VII, the French king at the time of Joan's birth, suffered from bouts of insanity and was often unable to rule. The king's brother Louis, Duke of Orléans, and the king's cousin John the Fearless, Duke of Burgundy, quarrelled over France's regency and the royal children's guardianship. The conflict climaxed with the assassination of the Duke of Orléans in 1407 on the orders of the Duke of Burgundy. Joan of Arc, also known as The Maid of Orléans, was born in 1412, the daughter of poor tenant farmers. She claimed to have received visions of the Archangel Michael, Saint Margaret, and Saint Catherine of Alexandria instructing her to support Charles VII and recover France from English domination late into the Hundred Years' War. Joan was sent to the siege of Orléans as part of a relief army and gained prominence after the siege was lifted only nine days later. Several additional swift victories led to Charles VII's coronation at Reims, a long-awaited boost to French morale that paved the way for the final French victory. On 23 May 1430, Joan was captured at Compiègne by a group of French nobles allied with the English and put on trial by the pro-English bishop Pierre Cauchon on various charges. She was burned at the stake on 30 May 1431, dying at the age of nineteen. In 1456, an inquisitorial court authorized by Pope Callixtus III re-examined the trial, pronounced her innocent, and declared her to be a martyr. In 1803, Napoleon Bonaparte defined her as the national symbol of France. Joan was beatified in 1909 and canonized in 1920. She is one of the nine secondary patron saints of France, along with Saint Denis, Saint Martin of Tours, Saint Louis, Saint Michael, Saint Rémi, Saint Petronilla, Saint Radegund and Saint Thérèse of Lisieux.

Péronne

Péronne is located at the confluence of the rivers Somme and Cologne, and its geographical location has been extremely important throughout its history. Few towns have been destroyed so often. Burned and pillaged in the time of the Normans, gravely damaged during the Spanish occupation, devastated by the Germans in 1870, totally destroyed in 1917 and finally bombarded and burned by the German air force in May 1940. In tune with this rather sad history, Péronne is also equally well known for its Monument to the Dead, the work of the architect Louis Faille, representing a Picardy woman with a clenched fist raised above the body of her son or husband killed by the war.

OF PARTICULAR INTEREST:

- Within the walls of the ancient château, the Historial de la Grande Guerre museum is a must for those interested in the Great Wars. Created in 1992 by architect Henri Ciriani, the building is characterised by the stark whiteness of the cement, inset with small cylinders, symbolic of military graves.

- The statue of Marie Fouré, a local heroine who apparently surprised, and then speared, one of Count Nassau's officers in 1536, resulting in his siege on the city being abandoned.

Doingt LXXIV Duin

A small village on the eastern outskirts of Péronne, Doingt is best known for its role in World War II. Doingt was captured by the 5th Australian Division on 5 September 1918, and the village was completely destroyed in the fighting. Also noteworthy is the Menhir of Doingt, one of northern France's largest and best-preserved Megaliths. Two local legends relate to the menhir. The first tells the story of two fairies from Rocogne's forest who came down to dance around it. The second describes the moment when the giant Gargantua found a stone in his shoe, which he removed and threw with such strength that it landed on the banks of the river Cologne.

The Life of Gargantua and of Pantagruel

Their story is a series of five novels written in the 16th century by François Rabelais. The adventures of two giants, Gargantua, the father and his son Pantagruel, are written in an amusing, extravagant and satirical vein. There is much crudity, scatological humour, and a large amount of violence, with long lists of vulgar insults filling several chapters. At the same time, Rabelais defines Pantagruelism (the philosophy of his giant Pantagruel) as "a certain gaiety of mind, pickled in the scorn of fortuitous things."

> *Readers, friends, if you turn these pages*
> *Put your prejudice aside,*
> *For, really, there's nothing here that's outrageous,*
> *Nothing sick, or bad — or contagious.*
> *Not that I sit here glowing with pride*
> *For my book: all you'll find is laughter:*
> *That's all the glory my heart is after,*
> *Seeing how sorrow eats you, defeats you.*
> *I'd rather write about laughing than crying,*
> *For laughter makes men human and courageous.*
> *BE HAPPY!*

The Department of Aisne

Aisne comprises parts of the former provinces of Île-de-France, Picardie and Champagne. The Aisne River crosses east to west, where it joins the Oise River and the landscape is dominated by rock masses with steep flanks. These rocks appear all over the region, but the most impressive examples are at Laon and the Chemin des Dames Ridge, so make sure you look out for them. Agriculture dominates the economy, especially cereal crops, resulting in vast tracts of the area being featureless and all too reminiscent of the Dust Bowl prairies. Nevertheless, silk and wool weaving still flourish in Saint-Quentin and other towns, which offers some variation and interest.

Saint-Quentin

The town is named after Saint Quentin, who is said to have been martyred there in the 3rd century. It is situated on the right bank of the Somme River, at its junction with the Canal de Saint-Quentin and was founded by the Romans in the Augustan period to replace the oppidum of Vermand as the capital of the Viromandui, the Celtic Belgian people who occupied the region. It received the name of Augusta Viromanduorum in honour of Emperor Augustus. During the early Middle Ages, a major monastery, now the Basilica of Saint-Quentin, was developed here based on the pilgrimage to the tomb of Saint Quentin. By the beginning of the 13th century, Saint-Quentin was a thriving city founded on its wool textile industry and as a centre of commerce, boosted by its position on the border of the kingdom of France. But from the 14th century, Saint-Quentin suffered from just this strategic position, enduring the French-English Hundred Years' War and then a siege by the Spanish army in 1557, ending with the looting of the city and its desertion for two years. Nevertheless, by the 19th century, Saint-Quentin had recovered to become a thriving industrial city, with textiles and mechanical products foremost among a wide variety of products. The First World War hit St Quentin very hard. The fighting destroyed 80% of buildings, and the reconstruction process was long. Its pre-1914 dynamism never fully reinstated.

OF PARTICULAR INTEREST:

- Saint-Quentin Town Hall overlooks the main Flemish-inspired central square and is adorned with 173 finely hewn sculptures illustrating scenes from the town's life. The Gothic Basilica of Saint-Quentin, built from the late 12th century to the late 15th century, houses the relics of St. Quentin.

Saint Quentin, the saint

Saint Quentin, also known as Quentin of Amiens, was an early Christian saint. The legend of his life is that he was a Roman citizen, the son of a man named Zeno, who had senatorial rank. Filled with apostolic zeal, Quentin travelled to Gaul as a missionary with Saint Lucian, who was later martyred at Beauvais. Quentin settled in Amiens and performed many miracles there, but because of his preaching, he was imprisoned by the prefect Rictiovarus. Quentin was manacled and tortured repeatedly but refused to renounce his faith. The prefect left Amiens to go to Reims, the capital of Gallia Belgica, where he wanted Quentin judged, but on the way, Saint-Quentin miraculously escaped and again started his preaching. Rictiovarus decided to interrupt his journey and pass the sentence. Quentin was tortured again, then beheaded and thrown secretly into the marshes around the Somme. Fifty-five years later, a blind woman named Eusebia, born of a senatorial family, came from Rome and miraculously discovered the body. The intact remains of Quentin came into view, arising from the water and emanating an odour of sanctity. She buried his body at the top of a mountain near Augusta Veromanduorum (now Saint-Quentin) and built a small chapel to protect the tomb, after which she recovered her sight. The life of bishop Saint Eligius reports that the exact place of the tomb was forgotten and that after several days of digging in the church, the bishop miraculously found it. Eligius distributed the nails with which Quentin's body had been pierced and some of the saint's teeth and hair. As a skilful goldsmith, he placed the relics in a shrine he had fashioned himself. He also rebuilt the church, now the Saint-Quentin Basilica.

The Hundred Years War

The Hundred Years' War was a series of armed conflicts fought between the kingdoms of England and France during the Late Middle Ages. It originated from English claims to the French throne initially made by Edward III of England and grew into a broader military, economic and political struggle involving factions from across Western Europe, fueled by emerging nationalism on both sides. The War typically described as taking place over 116 years was, in fact, an intermittent conflict that was frequently interrupted by external factors, such as the Black Death and several years of truces. The War is commonly divided into three phases separated by truces: the Edwardian War (1337–1360), the Caroline War (1369–1389), and the Lancastrian War (1415–1453). Each side drew many allies into the conflict, with English forces initially prevailing; however, the French forces under the House of Valois ultimately retained control over the Kingdom of France. The French and English monarchies thereafter remained separate, despite the monarchs of England (later Britain) styling themselves as sovereigns of France until 1802. During the War, five generations of kings from two rival dynasties fought for the throne of France, which was then the dominant kingdom in Western Europe. Tensions between the French and English crowns went back centuries to the origins of the English royal family, which was French in origin through William the Conqueror, the Norman duke who became King of England in 1066. English monarchs had, therefore, historically held titles and lands within France, which made them vassals to the kings of France. French monarchs systematically sought to check the growth of English power, stripping away lands as the opportunity arose, mainly whenever England was at War with Scotland, an ally of France. In the early years of the War, the English, led by their King and his son Edward, the Black Prince, saw resounding successes, but by 1378, under King Charles V the Wise and the leadership of Bertrand du Guesclin, the French had reconquered most of the lands ceded to King Edward in the Treaty of Brétigny (signed in 1360), leaving the English with only a few cities on the continent. In the following decades, the weakening of royal authority, combined with the devastation caused by the Black Death of 1347-1351 (which killed nearly half of France and 20-33% of England) and the significant economic crisis that followed, led to a period of civil unrest in both countries. These crises were resolved in England earlier than in France. The newly crowned Henry V of England seized the opportunity presented by the mental illness of Charles VI of France and the French Civil War between Armagnacs and Burgundians to revive the conflict. Overwhelming victories at Agincourt (1415) and Verneuil (1424) and an alliance with the Burgundians raised the prospects of an ultimate English triumph and persuaded the English to continue the War over many decades. A variety of factors prevented this, however. Notable influences include the deaths of Henry and Charles in 1422, the emergence of Joan of Arc (which boosted French morale), and the loss of Burgundy as an ally (concluding the French Civil War). The Siege of Orléans (1429) made English aspirations for conquest all but infeasible. Despite Joan's capture by the Burgundians and her subsequent execution, a series of crushing French victories concluded the siege, favouring the Valois dynasty. Notably, Patay (1429), Formigny (1450), and Castillon (1453) proved decisive in ending the War. England permanently lost most of its continental possessions, with only the Pale of Calais remaining under its control on the continent until the Siege of Calais (1558). By the War's end, feudal armies had mainly been replaced by professional troops, and aristocratic dominance had yielded to a democratisation of the manpower and weapons of armies. Although primarily a dynastic conflict, the War inspired French and English nationalism. The broader introduction of weapons and tactics supplanted the feudal armies, where heavy cavalry had dominated, and artillery became important. The War had a lasting effect on European history. Both sides produced innovations in military technology and tactics, including professional standing armies and artillery, that permanently changed European warfare.

Serancourt-le-Grand   LXXIII Martinwaeth

Seraucourt-le-Grand is a small town but also the crossing point for best known pilgrimage routes, the St James Way, the Via Francigena and Chemin Estelle, which traces a route between Saint Quentin and Paris.

Tergnier

Tergnier retains the traces of its 19th-century past as a main railway terminus. The Compagnie du Nord built a large housing estate in Tergnier to accommodate its workers, and the town grew, increasing from 154 inhabitants in 1793 to 3,536 in 1885. Since the Second World War, the town experienced a decline but has more recently shown signs of a renaissance. Now, visitors can find places to stay and visit.

OF PARTICULAR INTEREST:

- The Museum of the Resistance is dedicated to the resistance movement and the people deported from France.

Laon   LXXII Mundlothuin

The first sign of Laon as you approach will be the cathedral towers on the horizon, giving one a sense of how awestruck the Medieval travellers must have felt after days of walking or riding through woodland and open countryside. If today's pilgrims need a break, this is an endlessly fascinating place to take it. As the capital of the Aisne department, Laon occupies a dramatic site on top of a long ridge surrounded by wide plains. At the end of the 5th century, Remigius, Archbishop of Reims, instituted the bishopric of Laon. As a result, Laon became a principal town in the kingdom of the Franks, though possession of it was often disputed. Early in the 12th century, the communes of France set about emancipating themselves, and the history of the commune of Laon is one of the richest and most varied. The citizens had profited from Bishop Gaudry's temporary absence and failure to secure a communal charter, but on his return, he purchased the revocation of this document from the king of France and recommenced his oppressions. The consequence was a revolt in which the episcopal palace was burnt, and the bishop and several of his partisans were put to death. The fire spread to the cathedral and reduced it to ashes, but frightened by the success of their victory, the rioters went into hiding outside the town, which was then pillaged by the people of the neighbourhood, who were eager to avenge the death of their bishop. Later, during the Hundred Years' War, Laon was attacked and taken over by the Burgundians, who then gave it up to the English, only for it to be retaken by the French after the consecration of Charles VII. Finally, in 1870, an engineer blew up the citadel when the German troops were entering the town. Many lives were lost, and the cathedral and old episcopal palace were damaged. Today, the old town is best approached by the Poma, the only fully automated municipal cable car system in the world, which links the upper town (the historical) with the lower town.

OF PARTICULAR INTEREST:

- The Citadelle, a part of the old underground town, is now open to visitors and offers a fascinating subterranean wander through many epochs.
- Cathédrale de Notre Dame was completed in 1235 and was one of France's first major Gothic buildings, even predating the Notre Dame in Paris. Unfortunately, it lost two of its original seven towers during the Revolution. Look out for the 12th-century font, the painted relief of the Passion from the 14th century and a Serbian icon donated to the cathedral by Pope Urban IV in the 13th century.
- The Alms Hospital is the oldest of its kind in Northern France.
- Abbey Saint-Martin was an early Gothic church for the Premonstratensian order of canons. Although the building suffered some damage in 1944, it has since been fully restored and is worth discovering. Its unusually long nave, a classic Romanesque trait, proves that the church was built just as the Gothic style was being adopted. Look out for the beautifully carved oak pulpit from the 19th century and two Medieval recumbent tomb effigies, one of Jeanne de Flandres, a former abbess, and the other of Raoul II of Coucy.
- The Knights Templar chapel is particularly special because they are rare in France, and it is even rarer to see one in such good condition. The monument dates from 1140, about twelve years after the Templar order settled in the city, and would have

served as a funerary chapel. Look out for the mosaic floor. The peaceful flower garden around the chapel is where the cemetery used to be and is good for a minute or two of rest and reflection.

- Porte d'Ardon, where some pilgrims may have entered the town walls, has been an opening in the defences since the 10th century, though the current gate is from around the 1400s. Today's pilgrims use a different entrance but will leave through Porte de Soissons, built in the early 1200s. The best panoramas can be had from the old walls on the north and south sides of the high town. And Rempart Guillaume de Harcigny and the Promenade Yitzhak Rabin are highly recommended.

Premonstratensians

The Order of Canons Regular of Prémontré, also known as the Premonstratensians, the Norbertines and, in Britain and Ireland, as the White Canons, is a religious order of Canons of the Catholic Church founded in Prémontré, near Laon, in 1120 by Norbert of Xanten, who later became Archbishop of Magdeburg. Norbert was a friend of Bernard of Clairvaux and was largely influenced by the Cistercian ideals regarding his manner of life and the government of his order. As the Premonstratensians are not monks but Canons Regular, their work often involves preaching and exercising pastoral ministry. They frequently serve in parishes close to their abbeys or priories. Saint Norbert had made various efforts to introduce a strict form of canonical life in various communities of canons in Germany, but finally, he and thirteen companions established a monastery to be the cradle of a new order in a rural place called Prémontré. In 1126, there were nine houses when the order received papal approbation by Pope Honorius II. Others were established in quick succession throughout Western Europe, so by the middle of the 14th century, there were 1,300 monasteries for men and 400 for women. The Norbertines came to England in about 1143. Before the dissolution under Henry VIII, there were thirty-five houses. Still, like most orders, they were almost completely devastated by the successive onslaughts of the Reformation, French Revolution and Napoleon. At the beginning of the 20th century, there were twenty monasteries and one thousand priests. In the 21st century, Premonstratensians follow the Augustinian Rule and conduct small business enterprises such as cheese-making, breweries, retreat centres, and pilgrim accommodations to earn a living.

Abbey Vauclair

Abbey Vauclair is the perfect place for quiet reflection and rest. Formerly a Cistercian abbey, founded in 1134 by Saint Bernard of Clairvaux, it was built on a site already occupied by a church. Its east-west orientation led Bernard to name it Vauclair, reversing the name of the mother abbey (Clara Vallis). Supported by gifts from rich families, the abbey quickly prospered and was given several estates and farms. Fighting during the Hundred Years' War heavily damaged the structure, though it managed to survive until the French Revolution in 1789, when it was finally demolished and sold to the French state as a national property. Only ruins remain, but the grounds include an arboretum of apple and pear trees and a medicinal herb garden.

Corbeny   LXXI Corbunei

This small town intersects with the Chemin des Dames (Ladies' Way), which is thirty kilometres long and runs along a ridge between the valleys of the rivers Aisne and Ailette. The name dates back to the 18th century when Louis XV's daughters, Adelaide and Victoire, travelled to Château de La Bove, near Bouconville-Vauclair, on the far side of the

Ailette. The château belonged to Françoise de Châlus, former mistress of Louis XV, Countess of Narbonne-Lara and former Lady of Honour to Adelaide, whom the two ladies visited frequently. In an unusually generous move for a cuckolded husband,

the Count had the road surfaced to make their journey less arduous. The ridge's strategic importance first became evident in 1814, when Napoleon's young recruits beat an army of Prussians and Russians at the Battle of Craonne. Then, during World War I, the Chemin Des Dames lay in the part of the Western Front held by French armies, a position that led to several bloody battles between 1914 and 1918. There are numerous war memorials and cemeteries all along the route, German, French and British, and beneath the ridge there is La Caverne du Dragon (The Dragon's Lair), an almost one-kilometre square cave network, some twenty to thirty metres below the surface. These underground caverns were originally the result of limestone excavations for building purposes in the 17th century, but during World War I, they were used by both French and German forces as field hospitals and command posts, sometimes even simultaneously by both sides, though one suspects they were not aware of it at the time.

The Department of Champagne

As your route meanders through the vineyards of the Champagne region, it is worth remembering that these grapes will produce an elite French wine, determined by the exceptional nature of the soil. Most vineyards are situated halfway up the hillside, and the roots of the vine grow deep down into chalky depths covered by a thin layer of nutritious substances. The climate of the Champagne area also plays a major role. The

young vines must adapt to the dangers of frost in springtime and poor weather during the flowering period. Grape picking begins towards the end of September, about 100 days after the flowering of the vine, and involves a wealth of special preventive measures found only in this area. Picking is done by hand. The grape bunches are examined individually, and the green or damaged ones are discarded. The grapes' initial two or three rapid pressings produce the cuvée juice. Subsequent pressings give the premier taille and then the deuxieme taille. After this, any further juice of insufficient quality can become champagne. To produce its characteristic bubbles, Champagne has to undergo a process of double fermentation. During the first fermentation, the base wine, made from rather acidic grapes, is fermented in either stainless steel or, more traditionally, oak barrels. It is then siphoned off from the sediment and kept at colder temperatures to clear completely before being drawn off and blended with wines from other areas and years (except vintage champagne). The wine is bottled, and the liqueur de tirage (sugar, wine and yeast) is added. The bottles are stored in cool, chalky cellars for a year or more in the second fermentation. The yeast converts the sugar to alcohol and carbon dioxide, producing sparkle. The yeast cells die, leaving a deposit. To remove this, the inverted bottles are turned and tapped daily to shift the deposit into the neck. Finally, the deposits are expelled by the process known as dégorgement, and sugar is added to adjust the sweetness before the final cork is inserted.

Reims   LXX Rems

Renowned the world over by countless champagne labels, Reims is home to some of the best-known 'grandes marques', but the city has another, much earlier, claim to fame. Since the crowning of Clovis in 496 AD, most of the French monarchs have also been crowned in the remarkable Cathedral Notre Dame. A cathedral has stood on this site since 401, but the present building was begun in 1211 and survived the French Revolution and Two World Wars. Since then, twenty years of major restoration have taken place and continue. Christianity was established in Reims by the middle of the 3rd century, during which Saint Sixtus of Reims founded the Reims bishopric. By the 10th century, Reims had become a centre of intellectual culture thanks to Archbishop Adalberon, seconded by the monk Gerbert, who founded schools that taught the  Liberal Arts. In 1139, Louis VII granted the town a communal charter, but the Treaty of Troyes (1420) ceded it to the English, who had made a futile attempt to take it by siege in 1360. They were expelled on the approach of Joan of Arc, who in 1429 caused Charles VII to be consecrated in the cathedral. More recently, during World War II, General Eisenhower and the Allies received the unconditional surrender of the Wehrmacht in Reims. The only labyrinth on the Via Francigena is here in Reims. It was shaped like a complex square, with cut corners and sides, the paths separated by lines of dark blue stone. It covered the central part of the nave at the third and fourth spans and was made of soft stone that wore out beneath the feet of pilgrims. A distinctive aspect of the labyrinth was the inclusion of depictions of the master masons of the cathedral. In other churches and cathedrals, they are always left unknown and anonymous. The people in the corners of the labyrinth are successive master masons of the

cathedral, who are shown to be hard at work with tools in their hands. The person most responsible for the labyrinth's construction is generally identified as Aubry de Humbert, Archbishop of Reims, who decided, in 1211, to build a new cathedral in the place of the one destroyed by fire. Unfortunately, and surprisingly, the labyrinth was also destroyed by the Canons (priests charged with running the cathedral), who were disturbed by children playing on it during ceremonies. A plan to rebuild the labyrinth ran into technical and administrative difficulties and has since been replaced by a light projection on the ground, which plays only in the evening and during feast days. It was inaugurated on 19 September 2009.

OF PARTICULAR INTEREST:

- In Notre Dame Cathedral, excavations have shown that the present building occupies roughly the same site as the original one founded under the episcopacy of St Nicaise. This church was rebuilt during the Carolingian period and extended in the 12th century. In 1210, the cathedral was damaged by fire, and reconstruction started shortly after. In 1233, a long-running dispute between the cathedral chapter and the townsfolk (regarding taxation and legal jurisdiction) boiled over into open revolt. Several clerics were killed or injured during the resulting violence, and the entire cathedral chapter fled the city, leaving it under an interdict which effectively banned all public worship and sacraments. Work on the new cathedral was suspended for three years, only resuming in 1236. Construction then continued more slowly. The upper parts of the facade were finally completed in the 14th century, but apparently following 13th-century designs, giving Reims an unusual unity of style. Look out for the Great Rose window, which is best seen at sunset. The 13th-century window depicts the Virgin surrounded by apostles and angel musicians. The Nave, favourably compared with the nave in Chartres and renowned for its elegant capitals, is decorated with naturalistic flower motifs. The Smiling Angel is the most celebrated of the many that adorn the building. The Gallery of the Kings, a harmonious west façade decorated with over 2,300 statues, including fifty-six stone effigies of the French kings.

- Place Royale has a statue of Louis XV at its centre, and the Place Cardinal-Luçon has an equestrian statue of Joan of Arc.

- Porte de Mars is the oldest monument in Reims, and Mars Gate was one of four Roman gates to the city walls, restored at the time of the Norman Invasion of northern France in the 9th century. Look out for the mosaic displaying thirty-five medallions representing animals and gladiators.

- The Palace of Tau is the archbishop's palace adjoining the cathedral, and it was named after the T-shaped design based on early episcopal crosses. The palace, built in 1690 by Mansart and Robert de Coute, encloses a Gothic chapel, the 15th-century Salle du Tau and rooms associated with French coronations. On the eve of the coronation, the future king spent the night in the palace. After being crowned in the cathedral, he held a banquet in the Salle de Tau, with its magnificent barrel-vaulted ceiling and walls hung with 15th-century Arras tapestries. The palace now houses a museum of sculpture and tapestries from the cathedral, including a 15th-century tapestry of the baptism of Clovis, the first Christian king.

- The Surrender Museum is directly located on the spot where, on May 7, 1945, General Eisenhower and the Allies received the unconditional surrender of the Wehrmacht.

- Having visited the monuments and worked up a good thirst, this writer recommends stopping off at one of the Champagne houses, les grandes marques, which have their headquarters in Reims and some in the limestone caves.

Clovis

Clovis was the first king of the Franks to unite all of the Frankish tribes under one ruler, changing the form of leadership from a group of petty kings to rule by a single king and ensuring that the kingship was passed down to his heirs. He is considered to have been the founder of the Merovingian dynasty, which ruled the Frankish kingdom for the next two centuries. Clovis succeeded his father, Childeric I, as a king of the Salian Franks in 481 and eventually came to rule an area extending from what is now the southern Netherlands to northern France, corresponding in Roman terms to Gallia Belgica (northern Gaul). At the Battle of Soissons (486), he established  his military dominance of the rump state of the fragmenting Western Roman Empire, which was then under the command of Syagrius. By his death in 511, Clovis had conquered several smaller Frankish kingdoms in the northeast of Gaul, including some northern parts of what is now France. Clovis also conquered the Alemanni tribes in eastern Gaul and the Visigothic kingdom of Aquitania in the southwest. These campaigns added significantly to Clovis's domains and established his dynasty as a major political and military presence in Western Europe. Clovis is particularly significant because of his baptism in 508, largely due to the influence of his wife, Clotilde, who would later be venerated as a saint. Shortly before his death, Clovis called a synod of Gallic bishops to meet in Orléans to reform the Church and create a strong link between the Crown and the Nicene Christian episcopate. This was the First Council of Orléans. Thirty-three bishops assisted and passed 31 decrees on the duties and obligations of individuals, the right of sanctuary, and ecclesiastical discipline. These decrees, equally applicable to Franks and Romans, established equality between conquerors and conquered. After his death, Clovis was laid to rest in the Abbey of St Genevieve in Paris, but his remains were later relocated to Saint Denis Basilica. When Clovis died, his kingdom was partitioned among his four sons, Theuderic, Chlodomer, Childebert and Clotaire. This partition created the new political units of the Kingdoms of Rheims, Orléans, Paris and Soissons and inaugurated a tradition that would lead to disunity lasting until the end of the Merovingian dynasty in 751. When his grandchildren divided royal power 50 years after his death, Paris was kept as a joint property and a fixed symbol of the dynasty.

Saint-Martin-sur-le-Pré

Your route takes you through this little village, now partially subsumed by the outskirts of Chalons-en-Champagne, but it may nevertheless interest you to know that a prehistoric site dating back some 5,000 years was found near the village centre. Later, much later in the Middle Ages, St. Martin, then Bishop of Tours, travelled through the region and gave his name to the village. The word 'pré', meaning meadow, links back to the time when fertilised flood plains next to it produced a particularly lush grass that was used for common grazing.

Châlons-en-Champagne   LXIX Chateluns

Châlons-en-Champagne owes its name to the Gallic people of Châlons, who settled sixteen kilometres northeast of the present city. By 20 BC, the Romans had established a road network throughout ancient Gaul, including the Via Agrippa, the main route connecting Milan to Boulogne-sur-Mer, crossing the Marne at Châlons. Châlons-en-Champagne has preserved much of its past, as shown by its timber-framed facades and religious buildings. Set in the heart of the Champagne-Ardenne region in northeast France, Châlons-en-Champagne is the capital of the Marne department. It has long been a major economic hub in northern Europe, strategically located on the river Marne. Famous for its hillside vineyards, which produce the fine champagnes, and for the rolling countryside surrounding the town. Châlons is often referred to as Little Venice, and there has always been an artistic energy to the city. From the 9th century, Châlons became a prosperous market town trading agricultural produce with neighbouring regions. Outside the narrow Gallo-Roman walls surrounding the town, a square was created called the Place du Marché au Blé (the Corn Market) between the Nau and Mau rivers, known today as the Place de la République. Throughout the Middle Ages, the local industry was based on manufacturing high-quality woollen goods that were sold all over Europe. During the 18th Century, the city was extended, with the ramparts being replaced by boulevards, which formed the shape of the town that you see today. Construction included seventeen religious institutions and some outstanding architectural masterpieces. During the French Revolution, the historical name of Châlons-en-Champagne was changed to Châlons-sur-Marne because the name 'Champagne' reminded the bourgeoisie of the feudal system, which they hated. By World War I, Châlons was one of the main French garrison towns, but the city was not damaged despite being close to the enemy front line.

OF PARTICULAR INTEREST:

- The Cathedral of Saint-Etienne includes parts of the Romanesque building created in the 12th century. It was mainly rebuilt in Gothic, and two additional structures (in Baroque style) were added in the 17th Century.
- Notre-Dame-En-Vaux Collegiate church is listed as a World Heritage UNESCO site and has a carillon (peal) of fifty-six bells – one of the largest in Europe. It also has beautiful 16th-century stained glass windows and, in the museum, the remains of remarkable sculptures and statues used to decorate the former cloister.
- The Cirque is the old town circus completed in 1899, where the National Centre of Circus Acts is still housed.
- Le Couvent des Dames Régentes is a 19th-century convent and seminary that houses the School of Arts & Industry today. Many historic houses line the streets, particularly in the Rue de Chatillon, the Rue de la Marne, the Rue Gobet Boisselle and the Rue des Cordeliers.
- Jard Park, right in the heart of the city, is divided into three gardens, offering a natural environment to relax and enjoy the view.
- The Grand Jard, a French-style formal garden, is linked by a footbridge to the Jard Anglais on the canal's banks. The Petit Jard has a landscaped garden with an arboretum.

Fontaine-sur-Coole   LXVIII Funtaine

Fontaine-sur-Coole is located where the river, la Coole crosses Via Agrippa, a Roman road. It was absorbed into the Commune of Faux-Vésigneul in 1970, which is a union of the two villages of Faux and Vesigneul. A Roman legionary camp was discovered in the commune of Faux, on the Via Agrippa, and can be seen in aerial photographs from the Regional Archeology Service.

Via Agrippa

The Via Agrippa is any stretch of the network of Roman roads in Gaul/France built by Marcus Vipsanius Agrippa, to whom Octavian entrusted the reorganization of the Gauls. The Romans built 21,000 kilometres of roads in Gaul. At the Empire's peak no fewer than 29 great military highways radiated from the capital, Rome.

The Peutinger Map

The Peutinger road map accurately depicts the network of Roman roads that extended from the Atlantic coast of Europe to almost as far as India, and even indicates the existence of China. Roads are indicated in red ink with the mileage given for each segment of a zigzag path. Each segment of this path indicates a possible day's travel at the time, with inns, baths, and towns symbolized. While the road system was correctly drawn, topographical and geographical features were distorted and presented in a schematic form.

Donnement   LXVII Domaniant

Life in the village of Donnemont is documented from the Gallo-Roman era with the passage of the Langres Chalons road and the discovery of objects, including a sword, during excavations. Its name comes from the patron saint of the parish, Saint Amand. In 1196, the Donnement Hospital was united with the Hôtel Dieu in Troyes. The Saint Amand Church dates from the 12th/16th century. You can see a statue of Saint Amand in painted stone from the 16th century, a statue of Saint Nicolas, a 16th-century glass roof illustrating the Annunciation, and a large crucifix in wood and copper.

The Department of Aube

The Via Francigena is now crossing the department of Aube, perhaps best known for the 1932 visit of the late Turkish president Mustafa Kemal Ataturk, who signed a friendship treaty with France there. Named after one of the Seine's tributaries, Aube is predominantly an agricultural department, with arable land covering around a third of its surface. The northern and western parts are fairly mountainous, while the south and east contain fertile woodland. It is here that some of the finest wines are produced, such as Les Riceys, Bar-sur-Aube, Bouilly and Laines-aux-Bois. Aube has its own regional park called Foret d'Orient, a vast land of deep forests and secluded lakes.

Brienne-le-Chateau LXVI Breone

Spread along the right bank of the Aube, Brienne-le-Chateau is overlooked by an imposing château. Built during the latter half of the 18th century by the cardinal of Brienne, it houses an important collection of paintings, many of them historical portraits of the 17th and 18th centuries. The church dates from the 16th century and is best known for its impressive stained glass. A statue of Napoleon commemorates his sojourn in Brienne from 1779 to 1784 when he was studying at the military school.

Napoleon Bonaparte

Napoleon Bonaparte (15 August 1769 – 5 May 51821), France's general and first emperor, was born in Ajaccio, Corsica. Well-educated, he rose to prominence under the French First Republic and led successful campaigns against him, most notably in Italy. He took power in a coup d'état in 1799 and installed himself as First Consul. In 1804, he made himself emperor of the French people. As Emperor, Bonaparte fought a series of wars involving complex coalitions, both for and against him. After a streak of victories, France secured a dominant position in continental Europe, and Napoleon maintained the French sphere of influence through the formation of extensive alliances and the elevation of friends and family members to rule other European countries as French vassal states. His luck ran out, however, and the Peninsular War (1807–14) and the French invasion of Russia in 1812 marked major military failures. His Grande Armée was badly damaged and never fully recovered. In 1813, the Sixth Coalition defeated his forces at the Battle of Leipzig, and his enemies invaded France. Napoleon was forced to abdicate and was exiled to the Italian island of Elba. In 1815, he escaped and returned to power but was finally defeated at the Battle of Waterloo in June 1815. Bonaparte spent the last six years of his life in confinement by the British on the island of Saint Helena. An autopsy concluded he died of stomach cancer, but there has been debate about this, and some scholars have speculated that he was a victim of arsenic poisoning.

Bar-sur-Aube   LXV Bar

A pretty little town with architecture typical of the region, Bar-sur-Aube is most renowned as the birthplace of Gaston Bachelard, a postmaster who studied physics before finally becoming interested in philosophy. He was a professor in Dijon from 1930 to 1940 and then became the inaugural chair of history and philosophy of the sciences at the Sorbonne.

Gaston Bachelard

Bachelard was born on 27 June 1884. After leaving employment as a postal clerk, he studied physics and chemistry before becoming interested in philosophy. To obtain his doctorate (doctorat ès lettres) in 1927, he wrote two theses: Essai sur la connaissance approchée, under the direction of Abel Rey, and e, Étude sur l'évolution d'un problème de physique: la propagation thermique dans les solides, supervised by Léon Brunschvicg. Bachelard first taught from 1902 to 1903 at the college of Sézanne but turned  away from teaching to consider a career in telegraphy before finally moving towards science and mathematics. He was particularly fascinated by the great discoveries of the end of the 19th century and the beginning of the 20th century - radioactivity, quantum and wave mechanics, relativity, electromagnetism and wireless telegraphy. From 1930 to 1940, Bachelard was a professor at the University of Dijon and was appointed chair of the history and philosophy of science at the University of Paris in 1958. He died in Paris on October 16, 1962.

The Department of Haute-Marne

Haute-Marne is named after the Marne River. During World War II, Haute-Marne was partitioned under German occupation. The canal, which runs from the Marne to the Saône, was a border, dividing the department east and west. The east was a Reserved Zone, intended to create a new German state, whereas to the west would be the traditional Occupied Zone. Haute-Marne was finally liberated by the Allies in the form 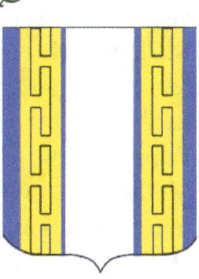 of the division of General Leclerc between August and September 1944.

Haute-Marne is well-known for some famous French great men and women:
- Louise Michel, a teacher and an important figure in the Paris Commune.
- Camille Flammarion, a prolific author of popular science works about astronomy, several notable early science fiction novels, and works on psychical research and related topics.
- The Goncourt brothers, most famous for the Prix Goncourt, a literature prize given by the Académie Goncourt for "the best and most imaginative prose work of the year".

The Goncourt brothers

Edmond de Goncourt (1822–1896) and Jules de Goncourt (1830–1870) were both French Naturalism writers who, as collaborative sibling authors, were also inseparable in life. They formed a partnership that is possibly unique in literary history because not only did they write all their books together, but they also did not spend more than a day apart during their adult lives until they were finally parted by Jules's death in 1870. The two brothers are known for their literary work and diaries, which offer an intimate view of the French literary society of the later 19th century. Their career as writers began with an account of a sketching holiday together. They then published books on aspects of 18th-century French and Japanese art and society. Their histories: (Portraits intimes du XVIIIe siècle (1857), La Femme au XVIIIe siècle (1862) and La du Barry (1878), are made entirely out of documents, autograph letters, scraps of costume, engravings and songs. In Portraits Intimes du XVIII siecle, they dismissed the vulgarity of the Second Empire in favour of a more refined age. When they came to write novels, it was with a similar attempt to give the inner, undiscovered, minute truths of contemporary existence. This included Germinie Lacerteux, based on the true case of their maidservant, Rose Malingre, whose double life they had never suspected. After her death, they found out that far from being an exemplary member of staff, she had been stealing from them, was an absinthe addict and had had a series of torrid affairs. Edmond and Jules are buried together (in the same grave) in Montmartre Cemetery. Edmond bequeathed his entire estate for the foundation and maintenance of the Académie Goncourt. Since 1903, the académie has continued to award the Prix Goncourt, which is probably the most important literary prize in French literature.

Nicolas Camille Flammarion

Flammarion (26 February 1842 - 3 June 1925) has been described as an "astronomer, mystic and storyteller" who was "obsessed by life after death, and on other worlds, and [who] seemed to see no distinction between the two" (James A. Herrick (2008). Scientific Mythologies: How Science and Science Fiction Forge New Religious Beliefs). Camille was born in Montigny-le-Roi, Haute-Marne, France and was the brother of Ernest Flammarion founder of the Groupe Flammarion publishing house. He went to Paris in 1856 as an apprentice engraver and took evening classes, particularly at the Association polytechnique. He then joined the Paris Observatory's calculation centre as a "student astronomer". But in 1862, his first book, 'La Pluralité des mondes habités' ('The Plurality of Inhabited Worlds'), caused a scandal when he claimed that other planets might be inhabited. Nevertheless, his books were very successful: 'Astronomie populaire' ('Popular Astronomy'), published in 1880, received an award from the Académie française and had sold 100,000 copies by 1900. Starting in 1865, he also taught classes and spoke at conferences, not only on astronomy but also on other subjects such as aeronautics. But above all, Flammarion was the most fascinated by the planet Mars. In 1876, he drew a map of the planet, taking into account his observations and those of all his predecessors since the 17th century. At the same time, the Italian astronomer Giovanni Schiaparelli claimed to have observed a network of canals on the surface of Mars, which Flammarion defended. These canals confirmed his theory that life was possible on Mars, even though he admitted that he had never observed them himself. In 1892, he published 'La Planète Mars et ses conditions d'habitabilité'. Astronomy is also very present in Flammarion's science fiction novels, 'Urania' and 'Stella', but his interest went beyond books. He installed a dome and a refracting telescope on a property in Juvisy-sur-Orge, which was given to him in 1882 by Louis-Eugène Méret, an admirer and amateur astronomer. On 28 January 1887, he founded the Société Astronomique de France (Astronomical Society of France) and became its president. When Flammarion died on 3 June 1925 in Juvisy, his peers named Asteroid 1021, discovered on 11 March 1924, Flammarion in his honour

Louise Michel

"It is true, perhaps, that women like rebellions. We are no better than men in respect to power, but power has not yet corrupted us."

Louise Michel was born on 29 May 1830 as the illegitimate daughter of a serving maid. She was raised by her grandparents, spent her childhood in the Château à Vroncourt la Cote and was provided with a libertarian education. When her grandparents died, she completed her teacher training. In 1865, Michel opened a school in Paris which became known for its modern and progressive methods. She corresponded with the prominent French romanticist Victor Hugo and began publishing poetry. During the Siege of Paris in November 1870, Michel became part of the National Guard. When the Paris Commune was declared, she was elected head of the Montmartre Women's Vigilance Committee and occupied a leading role in the revolutionary government of the Paris Commune. Women played a key role in the Paris Commune. They not only chaired committees but also built barricades and participated in armed violence. Michel ideologically justified a militant revolution, proclaiming, "I descended the Butte, my rifle under my coat, shouting: Treason! . . . Our deaths would free Paris." Michel would be among the few militants who survived the Paris Commune. In her memoirs, Michel confessed that the realities of the revolutionary government strengthened her resolve to end the discrimination against women. In December 1871, Michel was brought before the 6th Council of War, charged with offences including trying to overthrow the government, encouraging citizens to arm themselves, and herself using weapons and wearing a military uniform. Defiantly, she dared the judges to sentence her to death, saying, "It seems that every heart that screams for freedom has no other right than a bit of lead, so I claim mine!" Michel was sentenced to penal transportation and deported to New Caledonia. She remained there for seven years and befriended the local Kanak people. In 1880, amnesty was granted to those who had participated in the Paris Commune, and Michel returned to Paris, where her revolutionary passion was undiminished. She gave a public address on 21 November 1880 and continued her revolutionary activity in Europe, attending the anarchist congress in London in 1881, where she led demonstrations and spoke to huge crowds. While in London, she also attended meetings at the Russell Square home of the Pankhursts. She made a particular impression on a young Sylvia Pankhurst. In 1890, she was arrested again, and after an attempt to commit her to a mental asylum, she moved to London, where she opened the International Anarchist School for the children of political refugees. Michel returned to France in 1895 and died of pneumonia in Marseille on 10 January 1905. Her funeral in Paris was attended by more than 100,000 people. Michel's grave is in the cemetery of Levallois-Perret, in one of the suburbs of Paris. The grave is maintained by the community.

Clairvaux Abbey

Clairvaux Abbey is a good example of the general layout of a Cistercian monastery. A strong wall, furnished at intervals with watchtowers and other defences, surrounded the abbey precincts. Beyond it, a moat is artificially diverted from tributaries, which flow through the precincts, completely or partially encircled the wall. This water furnished the monastery with an abundant supply for irrigation and sanitation and for the offices and workshops. An additional wall, running from north to south, bisected the monastery into an inner and outer ward. The inner ward housed the monastic buildings, while the agricultural and other artisanal work was conducted in the outer ward. The precincts were entered by a gateway that opened onto barns, granaries, stables, workshops and workers' lodgings. A single gatehouse allowed communication through the wall, separating the outer from the inner ward. On passing through the gateway, the outer court conducted in the outer ward. The precincts were entered by a gateway that opened onto barns, granaries, stables, workshops and workers' lodgings. A single gatehouse allowed communication through the wall, separating the outer from the inner ward. On passing through the gateway, the outer court of the inner ward was entered, with the western façade of the monastic church in front. Immediately on the right of the entrance was the abbot's residence, close to the guest house. On the other side of the court were stables for the guests' horses and attendants' accommodation. The church occupied a central position with the great cloister to the south, surrounded by the chief monastic buildings. Further to the east, the smaller cloister contained the infirmary, novices' lodgings and quarters for the aged monks. The abbey of Clairvaux was converted into a prison in the 19th century, and, more precisely, the large cloister was used as a prison walk. The site of Clairvaux is one of the few testimonies in France of the transformation of monastic sites, places of voluntary confinement, into places of punitive confinement. The buildings preserve the marks of the occupation, first  by the monks and then by the prisoners. In 1971, two convicts, Claude Buffet and Roger Bontems, took as hostages a nurse and a prison guard. Buffet subsequently murdered them and said that he had done so because he wanted to die. Both prisoners were sentenced to death in June 1972 and were guillotined. On 16 January 2006, several detainees, having each spent from six to twenty-eight years in prison, signed a manifesto denouncing the false abolition of the death penalty. They declared that it had resulted in a slow and continuous punishment, a death in life, and called for restoration of the death penalty. They specifically denounced the French Republic's claim that the "enforcing of prison sentences... has been conceived not only to protect society and assure the punishment of the convict, but also to favour his amendment and prepare his rehabilitation". In contrast, they argued, "In reality, everything is for the punishment." Notable prisoners: the Russian anarchist Peter Kropotkin was imprisoned in Clairvaux between 1883 and 1886. Carlos the Jackal, an international terrorist, was transferred to Clairvaux in 2006.

St Bernard of Clairvaux

Born in 1090 at Fontaines, near Dijon, France, St Bernard died at Clairvaux in 1153. His parents both belonged to the highest nobility of Burgundy. Bernard, the third of a family of seven children, six of whom were sons, was educated with particular care because, while still unborn, a devout man had foretold his great destiny. At the age of nine, Bernard was sent to a renowned school in Chatillon-sur-Seine, kept by the secular canons of Saint-Vorles. He had a great taste for literature and devoted himself for some time to poetry. St. Robert, Abbot of Molesmes, had founded the monastery of Cîteaux, near Dijon, to restore the Rule of St. Benedict. Returning to Molesmes, he left the government of the new abbey to St. Alberic, who died in the year 1109. St. Stephen had just succeeded him (1113) as 3rd Abbot of Cîteaux when Bernard, with thirty young noblemen of Burgundy, sought admission into the order. Three years later, St. Stephen sent the young Bernard, at the head of a band of monks, to find a new house at Vallée d'Absinthe, or Valley of Bitterness, in the Diocese of Langres. This, Bernard named Claire Vallée of Clairvaux,

and as a result, the names of Bernard and Clairvaux became inseparable. The beginnings of Clairvaux Abbey were trying and painful. The regime was so austere that Bernard became ill, and only the influence of his friend, William of Champeaux, and the authority of the General Chapter could make him mitigate the austerities. The monastery, however, made rapid progress. Disciples flocked to it in great numbers and put themselves under the direction of Bernard. His father and all his brothers entered Clairvaux, leaving only Humbeline, his sister, and she, with her husband's consent, soon took the veil in the Benedictine convent of Jully. Gerard of Clairvaux, Bernard's older brother, became the cellarer of Citeaux. The abbey rapidly became too small for the number of people flocking there to enter religious life, making it necessary to send monks out to find new houses. As a result, the Monastery of the Three Fountains was founded in the Diocese of Châlons, Fontenay, in the Diocese of Autun and Foigny, in the Diocese of Laon.

Chateauvillain
In French, the word vilain can mean naughty or ugly, neither of which applies to this pretty little town dominated by its chateau.

Blessonville LXIV Blaecuile
Blessonville has been inhabited since the Neolithic period. The village was Gallo-Roman in Antiquity, and today, the thermal baths are still visible, and traces of ancient villas can be seen from the air.

Humes LXIII Oisma

Langres

Langres is situated on a hill at the northern end of the Langres Plateau. The town's walls contain a 2nd-century Roman gate, 15th to 16th-century towers, and other 16th to 18th-century gates. A stronghold of the Lingones, a Gallic tribe, Langres later became an important Gallo-Roman town called Andematunum. At the end of the 2nd century, St. Bénigne introduced Christianity to the town, and at the beginning of the 3rd century, St. Sénateur was the first bishop of Langres. From the 12th to the 18th century, the bishops of Langres, who had the title of duke, were ecclesiastical peers of the realm of France. The ramparts surrounding the town are about 3.5 kilometres long, can be walked around, and include seven fortified towers and seven gateways. Parts of the ramparts date back 2000 years, although some are much more recent. The citadel dates from the 19th century. Langres is also home to producers of an AOC-protected cheese of the same name.

OF PARTICULAR INTEREST:

- Denis Diderot's House of Enlightenment pays homage to Denis Diderot, born in Langres. This private mansion, from the 16th and 18th centuries, is dedicated to the philosopher and to his most famous work, the Encyclopédie, as well as to the Age of French Enlightenment.
- The statue of Denis Diderot in the centre of the town, in Place Diderot.
- The cathedral Saint-Mammes de Langres, built in the 2nd half of the 12th century, incorporates Roman and Gothic styles, with a little of each, and a facade rebuilt in the 18th century in the Classical style. The highlights in the cathedral include the carved stones, tapestries, ornamental stonework in the vaulted ceiling of the Chapel de la Sainte-Croix, added in the Renaissance period, and the treasury. The 13th-century cloister now houses the town library.

Denis Diderot (1713—1784)

"The first great writer who belonged wholly and undividedly to modern democratic society."

Diderot, a highly respected French literary critic was educated by the Jesuits but refused to enter one of the learned professions. He was turned adrift by his father and came to Paris, where he lived from hand to mouth for a time. Gradually, however, Diderot became recognised as one of the most powerful writers of the day. His first independent work was the Essai sur le mérite et la vertu (1745). As one of the editors of the Dictionnaire de Médecine, Paris, 1746), he gained valuable experience in the encyclopedic system. His Pensées Philosophiques, in which he attacked both atheism and the received Christianity, was burned by order of the Parliament of Paris.

In the circle of the leaders of the Enlightenment, Diderot became well-known for his Lettre sur les Aveugles (Letters on the Blind, London, 1749), which supported Locke's theory of knowledge. He attacked the conventional morality of the day and was imprisoned at Vincennes for three months, but gained his release with the influence of Voltaire's friend, Mme. du Chatelet, and remained in close relations with revolutionary thought leaders. Diderot made very little profit out of the Encyclopedie, and Grimm appealed on his behalf to Catherine of Russia, who, in 1765, bought his library, allowing him the use of the books for as long as he lived and assigning him a yearly salary, which she paid him for fifty years in advance. He lived, until his death, in a house provided by her. It was here (according to Grimm) that he wrote two-thirds of Raynal's famous Histoire Philosophique and contributed some of the most rhetorical pages to Helvetius's de l'esprit and Holbach's Systeme de la nature, Systeme social and Alorale Universelle. His numerous works include a variety of literary genres, from licentious tales and comedies, which pointed away from the stiff classical style of French drama to the most daring ethical and metaphysical speculations. Like his famous contemporary, Samuel Johnson, he is said to have been more effective as a talker than as a writer, and his mental qualifications were rather those of a stimulating force than of a reasoned philosopher. His position gradually changed from theism to deism, then to materialism, and finally, he rested in pantheistic sensualism.

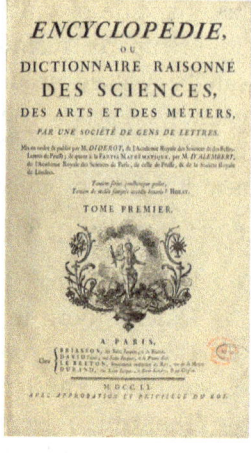

Grenant   LXII Grenant
The Department of Haute-Saône

Haute-Saône should be viewed as a transitional territory between several of the more depressed departments of eastern France and the so-called Blue Banana zone, characterised in recent decades by relatively powerful economic growth. The area is overwhelmingly rural, and in common with many rural departments in France, Haute-Saône has experienced a savage reduction in population and the absence of large towns and cities, which makes forward planning for the walking pilgrim an important factor.

Champlitte

Set on a rise, 240 metres above sea level, the territory of Champlitte is a crossroads for Champagne-Ardenne, Burgundy and Franche-Comté.

The origin of the name originates from Champlitte campus litensis or campus limites. Today, the inhabitants are known as the Chanitois. During the Roman Era, Champlitte was close to two major roads, one from Langres to Besançon, the other from Danmartin to Langres. Several villas have been found in the area, confirming that the area was inhabited.

OF PARTICULAR INTEREST:

- The castle and County Museum of Arts and Popular Traditions was officially founded in 1957. The museum owes its creation to the Demard family, who collected all sorts of furniture and equipment during the rural exodus and the modernisation of farms in the 50s. This is an ethnographic museum devoted to the life of a village in the late 18th century until the 20s.
- Champlitte is the largest wine-growing area in the department of Haute-Saône, and the Museum of Vine and Presses is housed in the Orangerie du Château.
- St Christophe church is renowned 15th-century belfry crowned with gargoyles.

Seveux LXI Sefui

Segobodium was the way station mentioned by the Antonine Itinerary, lying on the road from Vesontio (Besançon) to Andematunnum (Langres). The name survives as Seveux, the village at the point where the Roman road crosses the river on a bridge, and in the name Savoyeux, the village on the other bank. The two sites have yielded remains from the Roman period.

The Antonine Itinerary

The Itinerarium Antonini Augusti (The Itinerary of the Emperor Antoninus) is a famous register of the stations and distances along various roads. Seemingly based on official documents, possibly from a survey carried out under Augustus, it describes the roads of the Roman Empire. Almost nothing is known of its date or author, though scholars think it likely that the original edition was prepared at the beginning of the 3rd century. The British section is known as the Iter Britanniarum. The document has fifteen such itineraries, each applying to different geographic areas. The itinerary measures distances in Roman miles, where 1,000 Roman paces equals one Roman mile. However, Roman paces were not everywhere the same, and conversion to modern units is imprecise, but one Roman mile approximately equals 1,430 metres (0.89 miles).

Cussey sur l'Ognon   LX Cuscei

The etymology of this name comes from the Celtic word 'Cus', meaning rock. In 967, the village was called 'Cussiacus', and it was in 1269 that it took the name 'Cussey' before changing to 'Cuisens' in 1275 and gradually became Cussey sur l'Ognon from the Ognon River, was added. The discovery of a Neolithic polished axe proves that the site was occupied continuously during antiquity. The Romans built a ford across the Ognon, soon replaced by a bridge. The village is built around a castle built to watch over the bridge. When Christianity took root, Cussey passed to the Sainte-Bénigne abbey in Dijon, which handed it over to the metropolitan chapter of Besançon.

Besançon   LIX Bysiceon

Cradled in a loop of the river Doubs, at the foot of its towering citadel, the ancient city of Besançon is one of the best-preserved historic cities in France. In pre-Roman times, it was the capital of an area known as Sequania. When the Romans conquered the area, Julius Caesar described this naturally defensive site as the Jewel in my crown. Today, Besançon is the capital of the region of Franche Comté, a thriving university town and one of the most popular places in eastern France.

The centre of Besançon, known as la Boucle, the loop of the river, is a very well-preserved historic quarter, with no high-rise blocks or inappropriate modern developments, while the city's commercial and business hub has plenty of shops and restaurants. The whole of the old centre of Besançon is pedestrianised and has survived more or less intact. The old streets are lined with houses and buildings from the Renaissance to the early 20th century, built in the local two-coloured limestone.

OF PARTICULAR INTEREST:

- The Citadel is a UNESCO World Heritage site and a magnificent example of 17th-century military architecture designed by Vauban. Standing on a massive rock - sheer on both sides - the Citadel blocks the entrance to the loop of the river Doubs. As well as  being an important historic monument in its own right, the Citadel contains several museums, including a folk museum, a museum of the Resistance and the Deportation, an insectarium, and a zoo.

- St. Jean Cathedral is built on the ground plan of an earlier Carolingian cathedral, with an altar at both ends. It also houses one of the great works from Fra Bartolomeo, as well as an astronomic clock. Just outside the cathedral is the Porte Noire, a Roman triumphal arch, the principal vestige today of the Roman city that once stood on the site.

- The town centre of Besançon boasts two impressive museums, the most important being the Musée des Beaux-Arts, one of France's oldest provincial art galleries. The museum houses works by Cranach, Bronzino, Bellini, Reubens, Zurbaran, Goya, Fragonard, Courbet, Renoir, Bonnard, Signac, Marquet and Picasso.

- Besançon's second most important museum is the Museum of Time - a legacy of the city's watchmaking tradition - housed in the Renaissance Granvelle palace. The palace itself is one of the finest Renaissance townhouses in France, built for Cardinal Granvelle, who was chancellor to the Hapsburg emperor Charles V. It also contains a fine collection of 17th-century Bruges tapestries depicting the life of Charles V, still hanging in the room for which they were originally commissioned.
- The late 17th-century St. Jacques Hospital is still part of the Besançon University Hospital and contains one of the finest 18th-century pharmacies in France, preserved as a museum.

Notre-Dame des Buis

Built on a site with religious links since the 5th century, when St. Leonard, a hermit, took up residence in a cave nearby, the current Notre Dame des Buis chapel was built in the 17th century, damaged in 1815 and restored and enlarged in 1865. A simple construction, it nevertheless contains some interesting features such as the Bible dating from the 17th century, a Pietà (a subject in Christian art depicting the Virgin Mary cradling the dead body of Jesus) dating from the 14th century, and a small organ. The stained glass designs are inspired by the seasons.

St Leonard

Leonard was a Frankish noble in the court of Clovis I, founder of the Merovingian dynasty. He was converted to Christianity along with the king in 496 by Saint Remigius, Bishop of Reims. Leonard asked Clovis to grant him the right to liberate prisoners he considered worthy. He secured the release of many prisoners and later became the patron saint of prisoners. Later, he declined the offer of a bishopric and entered the monastery at Micy near Orléans, under the direction of Saint Mesmin and Saint Lie. Then, according to legend, Leonard became a hermit in the forest of Limousin, where he gathered some followers. Through  his prayers, the queen of the Franks safely bore a male child, and in recompense, Leonard was given royal lands at Noblac, near Limoges. According to another legend, prisoners who invoked him from their cells saw their chains break before their eyes. Many came to him afterwards, bringing their heavy chains and irons to offer them in homage. A considerable number remained with him, and he often gave them part of his vast forest to clear and use for growing crops so that they could feed and honestly provide for themselves.

Ornans

Roughly halfway between Pontarlier and Besançon, you will go through Ornans, an archetypal Franche-Comté town that has become the focal point of the valley. At this point, the river Loue is an abrupt trench with the water washing past the foundations of ancient balconied houses. Pierre Vernier, inventor of the eponymous gauge, and the painter Gustave Courbet were both born here.

OF PARTICULAR INTEREST:

- The Courbet museum

Gustave Courbet

"When I stop being controversial, I'll stop being important." Gustave Courbet was born in 1819 in Ornans, the eldest of four children and the only son of a close-knit and prosperous family. Courbet showed his affection for his family throughout his life and left behind many portraits of them, sometimes among the figures in his great compositions. He had a similar fondness for his native region, which he used as a background in several of his paintings. At around the age of fourteen, he was introduced to painting by père Baud, a teacher from Ornans and a former student of the Neo-Classical painter Gros. In 1837, the young man moved to Besançon and further honed his skills there. Courbet was twenty when he came to Paris to enrol in law school, but he soon gave up and followed his passion for painting. In 1848, Courbet had ten paintings accepted by the Salon and, from then on, achieved public recognition. However, some of Courbet's other works were greeted with total incomprehension and caused outrage, as in 1849 with The Stone Breakers (later destroyed). In the 2nd half of the 19th century, academic tradition required that large paintings should only have historical, biblical, mythological or allegorical subjects, but Courbet ignored this convention by painting a familiar domestic world on two vast canvases. The history of a burial at Ornans symbolises this point of view. Young Ladies by the Seine (Paris, Petit Palais), exhibited at the 1857 Salon, enabled Courbet to develop a circle of faithful admirers and defenders, and the commissions came flooding in. His abundant production encompassed a variety of subjects: hunting scenes, landscapes, and still lifes with flowers, among others. During this same period, Courbet painted his provocative work, The Origin of the World (1866), a private commission that was to remain hidden from public view for a long time. In April 1871, the Executive Committee for the Commune de Paris gave him the task of reopening the galleries in Paris and organising the Salon. Although elected to the Council of the Commune, Gustave Courbet was not in the National Guard but was nevertheless arrested on 7th June by the Versailles government forces. In September, he was sentenced to six months in prison and fined 500 francs, with 6,850 francs added for legal costs. The sentence was quite lenient compared to the death penalties and deportations given out to other communards, but that was only the beginning of his legal difficulties.

On 12th April 1871, the Commune voted to demolish the Vendôme column on 16th May 1871, and Courbet was ordered to pay the costs of reconstructing it by the government of the National Defence. He did, but then moved to Switzerland, fearing further imprisonment. During his exile, Courbet began drinking heavily and rarely produced works worthy of his talent. He died on 31st December 1877, a few days after the contents of his Paris studio had been dispersed at a public sale.

Mouthier-Haute-Pierre

The route now takes you up mountains and through valleys. Mouthier-Haute-Pierre is the last village before the gorge Nouailles and offers fantastic views over the gateway to Switzerland. The village was founded by a small religious order that cleared the hillsides, planted vines and eventually built an abbey that was to become one of the largest in Gaul. Cardinal de Granvelle rebuilt nine priory houses, which can still be seen today.

OF PARTICULAR INTEREST:

- St. Lawrence church was built on the edge of the priory cemetery in 1390 and enlarged between 1550 and 1581, thanks to donations of Cardinal Granvelle. The Cardinal

went on to build the tower, which peaks at 43 meters.
- The famous cherry kirsch is made from the cherries grown in orchards, which you will see on the hillsides around the village.

The Department of Doubs

As early as the 13th century, inhabitants of the northern two-thirds of Doubs spoke Franc-Comtois, a dialect of Langue d'Oïl. Residents of the southern third of Doubs spoke a dialect of the Arpitan language. Both languages co-existed with French, the official language of law and commerce, and continued to be spoken frequently
in rural areas into the 20th century. They are both still spoken today, but not daily. Doubs was important as a portal to Switzerland through the pass at Joux. Many famous people, including Mirabeau, Toussaint Louverture and Heinrich von Kleist, were imprisoned in the Château de Joux. It is also the birthplace of the automotive manufacturer Peugeot.

Nods   LVIII Nos
Pontarlier   LVII Punterlin

Pontarlier occupies the ancient Roman station of Ariolica in Gallia and is located on the road from Urba (modern Orbe, Canton Vaud, Switzerland) to Vesontio (modern Besançon). After the Burgundian invasion in the 5th century, Pontarlier became an unavoidable trade route from the kingdom of Burgundy to Switzerland, Germany or Lombardy. Until the 17th century, crossing the Jura mountains was the easiest way. The city of Pontarlier is briefly mentioned in Victor Hugo's Les Misérables when the convict Jean Valjean has to report for his parole after being released from the galleys. Breaking these instructions is a major turning point in the novel and creates a major conflict for Valjean later in the story. Pontarlier is also the gateway to a very large protected nature area, where the forest, the lakes and the green pastures are indispensable to the manufacture of the Mont d'Or cheese.

OF PARTICULAR INTEREST:

- Distillerie GUY is the last distillery of Absinthe in Pontarlier and a family business for 5 generations (since 1890).
- The triumphal arch of the Porte Saint-Pierre (18th century) was built in 1771 following the plans of military engineer Jean Lemichaud d'Arçon.
- The church of St Bénigne is most famous for its contemporary stained glass work designed by Manessier.

Victor Hugo

(26 February 1802 – 22 May 1885) Famous worldwide as both a literary and political celebrity, Victor Hugo succeeded in the difficult task of being both intellectually respectable and, at the same time, immensely popular, especially through two of his major works, Notre Dame de Paris and Les Misérables. Hugo was born in Besançon and, by the age of 13, realised he had a literary calling. His early poems won several awards, including two mentions from the Academie Francaise.

During the 1820s, he became one of the leading figures of the French Romantic movement. In 1830, his position was enhanced by the success of the play Hernani, which was subject to fierce controversy, symbolising as it did the conflict between new Romantic ideas and classical French theatre. In 1841, he was elected (at the fifth attempt) to the Academie Francaise, but following the failure of his play Les Burgraves, Hugo turned his attention to public and political issues, becoming a Peer of France in 1845. Tragedy also struck during this period when, in September 1843, his daughter Léopoldine and her husband were drowned in the Seine. By July 1851, his opposition to Louis Bonaparte

had hardened with his coining of the phrase, "We have had Napoleon the Great, now we have to have Napoleon the Small", and after the coup d'état of the 2nd December, which he tried in vain to oppose, he fled the country to avoid arrest. Although legally able to return to France in 1859, Hugo defiantly decided to stay in Guernsey, where he wrote, completed or published most of the works for which he is best known. Following the fall of Louis Bonaparte in 1870, Hugo returned to France as a hero and once more took an interest in political life. A believer in European integration, he planted an oak tree (which still flourishes today) in the garden of Hauteville House, predicting that when the tree was mature, The United States of Europe, uniting all European nations, would have become a reality. Hugo's wish was to be buried in a pauper's coffin. While this wish was granted, he was nevertheless given a National Funeral. The coffin lay in state under the Arc de Triomphe, and on the 1st of June 1885, he was buried as a national hero in the Panthéon. It is estimated that at least two million people followed the funeral procession.

Absinthe

Absinthe is an anise-flavoured spirit derived from herbs, including the flowers and leaves of the herb Artemisia absinthium (Wormwood). Absinthe originated in the canton of Neuchâtel in Switzerland and achieved great popularity as an alcoholic drink in late 19th and early 20th century France. Due partly to its association with bohemian culture, Absinthe was opposed by social conservatives and prohibitionists. Charles Baudelaire, Paul Verlaine, Arthur Rimbaud, Henri de Toulouse-Lautrec, Amedeo Modigliani, Vincent van Gogh, Oscar Wilde, Aleister Crowley and Alfred Jarry were all notorious bad men of the day, who were devotees of the Green Fairy. Absinthe has been portrayed as a dangerously addictive psychoactive drug. The chemical thujone, present in small quantities, was singled out and blamed for its alleged harmful effects. By 1915, Absinthe had been banned in the United States and most European countries, except the United Kingdom, Sweden, Spain, Portugal, Denmark and the Austro-Hungarian Empire. Although Absinthe was vilified, no evidence has shown it to be more dangerous than ordinary spirits. Its psychoactive properties, apart from those of alcohol, have been much exaggerated.

Pastis

Pastis is an anise-flavoured liqueur first commercialised by Paul Ricard in 1932, some seventeen years after the Absinthe ban. By legal definition, Pastis is often associated with its historical predecessor, Absinthe, but the two are, in fact, very different. Pastis does not contain Wormwood. Furthermore, it has the distinct flavour of liquorice root (another herb of Asian origin), which is not a part of a traditional Absinthe. Where bottled strength is concerned, traditional Absinthes were bottled at 45-74% ABV (alcohol by volume), while Pastis is typically bottled at 45-50% ABV. Finally, unlike traditional Absinthe, Pastis is a liqueur that is always bottled with sugar.

Jougne   LVI Antifern

For some years, the modern Via Francigena passed from Pontarlier Via Sainte Croix to Yverdon-les-Bains before returning to the historic town of Orbe. It is now understood that this was an error in interpreting the name of Antifern from Sigeric's chronicle and referred to the border town of Jougne (LVI), which lies at the western end of the ridge still today known as la côte de l'Entefer. You will see the many names associated with producing and using iron (Ferrum - in Latin) - La Ferrière, Les Fourgs and rue des Forges in Jougne. The iron-rich soils, coal from the Jura and water from the Jougnena River gave birth to an iron industry in the valley as early as 300 B.C. The nearby town of Vallorbe is known as the Iron City of Switzerland and boasts an iron and railway museum. Jougne straddles the former Roman road connecting Orbe, Pontarlier, and Besançon - a section of the road showing scars of passing chariots and carts is still visible near Chez Barrat a little after the border crossing. The strategic position of Jougne made it an ideal location to extract tolls from travellers, a role that it played into the Middle Ages, while pilgrims would rest in the town when travelling between the abbeys of Saint-Maurice in Valais and the Cluniac monasteries of France. The crypt of the la Chapelle Saint-Maurice, beside the path on the southern side of the town, dates from the 9th century and was part of a priory which perhaps could have been the stopping place for Archbishop Sigeric. The chapel itself dates from the 12th century. The relics of Saint-Maurice can be found today in the Jougne parish church, which has been dedicated to himTo the west of the Jougnena is Mont d'Or, famous for the railway tunnel linking France and Switzerland and for the delicious cheese that bears its name.

Switzerland

HELVETIA

The Swiss Alps

Yesterday brown was still thy head, as the locks of my loved one,
Whose sweet image so dear silently beckons afar.
Silver-grey is the early snow to-day on thy summit,
Through the tempestuous night streaming fast over thy brow.
Youth, alas, throughout life as closely to age is united
As, in some changeable dream, yesterday blends with today.

Johann Wolfgang von Goethe

Despite being one of the most visited countries in Europe, Switzerland remains one of the least understood. The landscape ranges from 643 feet above sea level in Ascona to 15,199 feet above sea level on The Dufour Peak. It has over 1,500 lakes, meaning you will never be more than ten kilometres from one. Not surprisingly, 60% of Switzerland's electricity is produced by hydroelectric power. Faced with an ever-increasing onslaught of visitors, the Swiss are content to abide by a quaint stereotype that's easily packaged and sold – the familiar Alpine idyll of cheese, chocolate, clocks, Heidi and the Matterhorn, while keeping the best bits for themselves. The other Switzerland – the one the Swiss inhabit – needs time and patience to find, but it can be an infinitely more rewarding place to explore. Within this rugged environment, community spirit is perhaps stronger than anywhere else in Europe. Since the country is not an ethnic, linguistic or religious unity, it has survived – so the Swiss are fond of saying – simply through the will of its people to resolve their differences. Switzerland has four national languages - French, German, Italian and Rhaeto-Romantsch. However, Swiss people value their shared Swissness and cherish their hometown identity and their differences from their neighbours. Tensions exist between the four language communities, as they do between Catholic and Protestant or between urban and rural areas, while regional characteristics remain sharply defined and diverse. The three great Swiss cities of Geneva, Zürich and Basel are crammed with world-class museums and galleries. In Zürich and Lausanne, a humming arts scene and underground club culture feed nightlife as vibrant as anything you'll find in much larger European cities. The Alps and their foothills dominate the landscapes, but mountains aren't the only story. In the north and centre are lush, rolling grasslands, epitomised by the velvety green hills of the Emmental and traditional dairy-farming country. Vineyards rise tiered above Lake Geneva, the Rhône Valley and the Rhine. The southeast is cut through by wild, high-sided valleys, lonely, dark and thickly forested. Most surprisingly, bordering Italy in the south, you'll find subtropical Mediterranean-style flower gardens, sugarloaf hills and sunny, palm-fringed lakes.

Vaud

Vaud is the first canton the Via Francigena will traverse in Switzerland. Vaud was inhabited in prehistoric times, and later, the Celtic tribe of the Helvetii took over until Caesar's troops defeated it in 58 BC. Vevey (Viviscus) and Lausanne (Lausonium or Lausonna) are just two of the many towns established by the Romans. In 27 BC, the state of Civitas Helvetiorum was established around the capital of Aventicum, and there are still many Roman remains in the town today. Between the 2nd and the 4th centuries, the area was repeatedly invaded by Alemannic tribes, and in the 5th century, the Burgundians occupied the area. The Merovingian Franks later replaced the Burgundians, but their occupancy did not last long either, and in 888, the area of the Canton of Vaud was made part of the Carolingian Empire. It was only under the Counts of Savoy that the area was finally given political unity, but as the power of the Savoys declined at the beginning of the 15th century, the land was occupied by troops from Bern, and by 1536, the area was completely annexed. The reformation was started by co-workers of John Calvin, but it was only decisively implemented when Bern put its full force behind it. In 1723, Major Abraham Davel led a revolt in protest at what he saw as the denial of political rights for the French-speaking Vaudians by the German-speaking Bernese. He was subsequently beheaded, but undeterred by his cruel fate, the Vaudians drove out the Bernese governor and declared the Lemanic Republic. Vaud became the canton of Léman, which, in 1803, joined the re-installed Swiss confederation, and despite Bernese attempts to reclaim Vaud, it has remained a sovereign canton ever since. In the 19th century, the canton of Vaud was an outspoken opponent of the Catholic separatist movement (Sonderbund), which led to intervention in 1847 by 99,000 Swiss Federal troops under General Henri Dufour, against 79,000 separatists in what is called the Sonderbund War. Separation was prevented at the cost of very few lives. Today, Vaud is a highly diversified region, offering culture in towns like Lausanne and its Chasselas grapes, making it Switzerland's second most important wine canton. The perpendicular terraced vineyards plunge from hillside villages right down to the edge of Lake Geneva, making this writer wonder how on earth they are harvested.

Orbe   Lv Urba

In the Middle Ages, Orbe sat on the road over the Jougne Pass and at the crossroads of two major transportation routes. One stretched from the Jura Mountains to the Alps, while the other ran from the Rhine River to the Rhone River. The municipality grew on both sides of the Orbe, and at some point, a bridge was built across the river that joined the two settlements. The town remained part of the independent Kingdom of Arles or Burgundy until the death of Rudolf III in 1032. Land and rights in the town passed through several nobles, but a record from 1183 shows that the town's churches and much of the land were owned by the Baulmes and Payerne Priories. Around the end of the 11th century, Romainmôtier Abbey acquired some land in the town, on which they built a hospital, which later expanded into the nearby Notre-Dame chapel.

OF PARTICULAR INTEREST:
- The Gallo-Roman villa known for its Roman mosaics, which are composed of several hundreds of pieces on the floor of the original site. The villa, built around AD 160, was a palace belonging to a rich but unknown landowner. Nowadays, eight mosaics are still visible and can be visited.

Lausanne   LIV Losanna

A perfect place to take a break and enjoy the pleasant shore walks. There has been a settlement on the hill of Lausanne since at least the Stone Age, but most city histories trace its origin to the Roman camp Lausanna, which occupied a position just down the hill toward the lake in what is now the village of Vidy. Relocated to a more defensible hilltop in the Middle Ages, Lausanne's increasing wealth and importance were largely derived from its placement on the primary north-south routes between Italy and the North Sea. Today, the town is built on three hills, surrounded by vineyard-covered slopes, with Lake Geneva at its feet. It also is part of the Swiss Riviera that stretches to Montreux and the eastern end of the lake, an area that has been a second home to writers, artists and musicians for over 150 years, starting with the Shelleys and Lord Byron (Frankenstein is rumoured to have been written here). Other famous residents included Ernest Hemingway and Charlie Chaplin, who lived in Vevey from the mid-1930s. There are too many museums and places of interest to list, but here are some of particular interest:

- Notre Dame de Lausanne is Switzerland's most impressive piece of early Gothic architecture. It was built in several stages, with the first builder beginning construction work in 1170 using Roman materials. Twenty years later, the present church was built, a project that did not end until 1215. From then on, Jean Cotereel, the third builder, continued work on the site by constructing the western section, giving it a porch and two towers, one with a belfry, while the other remained uncompleted. It was only in 1275 that the cathedral was finally consecrated by both Emperor Rudolph of Hapsburg and Pope Gregory X. In 1536, the cathedral underwent significant changes during the Reformation when a new liturgical area was built in the nave. After that, it was restored several times in the 18th century and again in the 19th century under the leadership of the famous French architect Eugène-Emmanuel Viollet-le-Duc. Look out for the multi-coloured interior, which was covered over during the Reformation and then revealed at the beginning of the 20th century. The paintings are still visible in the Chapel of the Virgin and on the statues of the painted doorway, which is unique in all of Europe and has been completely restored since October 2007. The rose window depicts the Medieval view of the world arranged around the figure of God the creator.

- The Olympic Museum houses permanent and temporary exhibits relating to sport and the Olympic movement – the largest archive of the Olympic Games in the world.
- Beaulieu Castle is one of the city's most majestic private 18th-century buildings. In 1766, the estate was acquired by the pastor Gabriel-Jean-Henry Mingard, also the son-in-law of the mayor of Amsterdam. Since 1976, the Beaulieu chateau has housed the Collection de l'Art Brut, which has been built up since the original donation of the personal collection of the French artist Jean Dubuff. The artists are mainly European but also from North America, South America, Africa and Asia.
- The Musée de l'Elysée photo museum houses eight exhibition rooms over four floors, a bookshop, a reading room and more than 100,000 original prints. Its international exhibition programme covers many photographic styles and techniques, both past and present.

Lord Byron

George Gordon Byron, 6th Baron Byron (22 January 1788 – 19 April 1824) was an English poet and one of the major figures of the Romantic movement. Among his best-known works are the lengthy narratives Don Juan and Childe Harold's Pilgrimage. Byron was educated at Trinity College, Cambridge before he travelled extensively across Europe to such places as Italy, where he lived for seven years in Venice, Ravenna, and Pisa after he was forced to flee England due to threats of lynching. He frequently visited his friend and fellow poet Percy Bysshe Shelley during his stay in Italy.

His one child, conceived within marriage, Ada Lovelace, was a founding figure in computer programming based on her notes for Charles Babbage's Analytical Engine. Byron was sent to Harrow School in 1801 but also fell in love with Mary Chaworth. When he refused to return to Harrow in September 1803, his mother wrote, "He has no indisposition that I know of but love, desperate love, the worst of all maladies in my opinion. In short, the boy is distractedly in love with Miss Chaworth." Byron spent three years at Trinity College, engaging in boxing, horse riding, gambling, and sexual escapades. While at Cambridge, he also formed lifelong friendships with men such as John Cam Hobhouse, who initiated him into the Cambridge Whig Club, which endorsed liberal politics, and Francis Hodgson, a Fellow at King's College, with whom he corresponded on literary and other matters until the end of his life. Byron became a celebrity after the publication of the first two cantos of Childe Harold's Pilgrimage (1812). On the initiative of the composer Isaac Nathan, he produced in 1814–1815 the Hebrew Melodies (including what became some of his best-known lyrics, such as "She Walks in Beauty" and "The Destruction of Sennacherib". But, involved at first in an affair with Lady Caroline Lamb and with other lovers and also pressed by debt, he began to seek a suitable marriage, considering – amongst others – Annabella Millbanke. However, in 1813 he met for the first time in four years his half-sister, Augusta Leigh. Rumours of incest surrounded the pair. Augusta's daughter Medora was suspected to have been Byron's child. To escape from growing debts and rumours, Byron pressed in his determination to marry Annabella, who was said to be the likely heiress of a rich uncle. They married on 2 January 1815, and their daughter, Ada, was born in December of that year. However, Byron's continuing obsession with Augusta Leigh (and his continuing sexual escapades with actresses such as Charlotte Mardyn and others) made their marital life miserable. Annabella considered Byron insane, and in January 1816, she left

him, taking their daughter, and began proceedings for a legal separation.

Their separation was made legal in a private settlement in March 1816. The scandal of the separation, the rumours about Augusta, and ever-increasing debts forced him to leave England in April 1816, never to return. Later in life, Byron joined the Greek War of Independence to fight the Ottoman Empire, for which Greeks revere him as a folk hero. He died leading a campaign in 1824, aged 36, from a fever contracted after the first and second sieges of Missolonghi.

Charlie Chaplin

"I was hardly aware of a crisis because we lived in a continual crisis, and, being a boy, I dismissed our troubles with gracious forgetfulness."

Charles Spencer Chaplin (16 April 1889 – 25 December 1977) was an English comic actor, filmmaker, and composer who rose to fame in the silent film era. He became a worldwide icon through his screen persona, the Tramp, and is considered one of the film industry's most important figures. His career spanned over 75 years, from childhood in the Victorian era until a year before he died in 1977. Chaplin's childhood in London was poor. His father was absent, his mother struggled financially, and he was sent to a workhouse twice before the age of nine. When he was 14, his mother was committed to a mental asylum. Chaplin began performing early, touring music halls and later working as a stage actor and comedian. At 19, he was signed to the Fred Karno company, which took him to the United States. He was scouted for the film industry and began appearing in 1914 for Keystone Studios. He soon developed the Tramp persona and attracted a large fanbase. He directed his own films and continued to hone his craft as he moved to the Essanay, Mutual, and First National corporations. By 1918, he was one of the world's best-known figures. In 1919, Chaplin co-founded the distribution company United Artists, which gave him complete control over his films. His first feature-length film was The Kid (1921), followed by A Woman of Paris (1923), The Gold Rush (1925), and The Circus (1928). He initially refused to move to sound films in the 1930s, producing City Lights (1931) and Modern Times (1936) without dialogue. His first sound film was The Great Dictator (1940), which satirised Adolf Hitler. *"I wanted everything to be a contradiction: the pants baggy, the coat tight, the hat small, and the shoes large... I added a small moustache, which, I reasoned, would add age without hiding my expression. I had no idea of the character. But the moment I was dressed, the clothes and the makeup made me feel the person he was. I began to know him, and by the time I walked on stage he was fully born."*

The 1940s were controversial for Chaplin, and his popularity declined rapidly. He was accused of communist sympathies, and some members of the press and public were scandalised by his involvement in a paternity suit and marriages to much younger women. An FBI investigation was opened, and Chaplin was forced to leave the US and settle in Switzerland. Chaplin founded a new production company, Attica, and used Shepperton Studios for the shooting. In the last two decades of his career, Chaplin concentrated on re-editing and scoring his old films for re-release and securing their ownership and distribution rights. In an interview he gave in 1959, the year of his 70th birthday, Chaplin stated that there was still "room for the Little Man in the atomic age". Chaplin had a series of minor strokes in the late 1960s, which marked the beginning of a slow decline in his health. Although he still had plans for future film projects, by the mid-1970s, he was very frail. He experienced several further strokes, which made it difficult for him to communicate, and he had to use a wheelchair. In the 1975 New Year Honours, Chaplin was awarded a knighthood by Queen Elizabeth II, though he was too weak to kneel and received the honour in his wheelchair. In the early morning of Christmas Day 1977, Chaplin, aged 88, died at home after having a stroke in his sleep. He was interred in the Corsier-sur-Vevey cemetery on 1 March 1978, but his coffin was dug up and stolen from its grave by Roman Wardas and Gantcho Ganev. The body was held for ransom in an attempt to extort money from his widow, Oona Chaplin. The pair were caught in a large police operation in May, and Chaplin's coffin was found buried in a field in the nearby village of Noville. It was re-interred in the Corsier cemetery in a reinforced concrete vault.

Vevey LIII Vivaec

A settlement has existed here from as early as the 2nd millennium BC. Under Rome, it was known as Viviscus or Vibiscum and mentioned for the first time by the ancient Greek astronomer and philosopher Ptolemy, who named it Ouikos. In the Middle Ages, it was an important station on the Via Francigena, ruled by the diocese of Lausanne. Today, Vevey is a holiday resort, wine-trading centre, and corporate headquarters for Nestlé. The Riviera town has long been popular with British and European celebrities.

OF PARTICULAR INTEREST:

- The Swiss Camera Museum covers the history of photography, from the camera obscura and magic lantern to the latest numerical images. If possible (and if you like jazz), try to time your journey to coincide with the nine-day Cully Jazz Festival, which takes place on the lakefront in early April.
- Alternatively, you could aim for the August Street Artists Festival, which draws 1,200 jugglers, mimes, puppeteers and other performers.

Walking along the banks of Lake Geneva today is nothing like the experience our pilgrim forebears would have had. In Roman times, the city's situation on the northeast shore of Lake Geneva and at the fork in the Roman road from Italy over the Simplon Pass made it an important settlement, but there is very little to see of this part of its history. Today, it is a trail of sophisticated and upmarket suburbs set against the stunning backdrop of the Swiss Alps. The climax of this particular phase of today's Via Francigena route is in Montreux.

Montreux

Montreux lies on the northeast shore of Lake Geneva at the fork on the Roman road from Italy over the Simplon Pass, where the roads to the Roman capital of Aventicum and the road into Gaul through Besançon are separated. This made it an important settlement in the Roman era. In the 12th century, viticulture was introduced to the region, and the sunny slopes of the lake from Lavaux to Montreux became an important wine-growing region. The Reformation made the region around Montreux and Vevey an attractive haven for Huguenots from Italy, who brought their artisanal skills and set up workshops and businesses. In 1798, Napoleon liberated the region from the Bernese, and in the 19th century, the tourist industry became a major commercial outlet, which continues today.

OF PARTICULAR INTEREST:

- Château de Chillon, Switzerland's most visited historical building, was originally owned by the House of Savoy. The Castle houses several Medieval frescoes and Gothic dungeons, the latter of which were the subject of a poem by Lord Byron: The Prisoner of Chillon. The poet directly references the château in the line: "There are seven pillars of Gothic mould/In Chillon's dungeons deep and old…"
- The Montreux Jazz Festival has a world-famous reputation for its diverse and renowned musical performances. Although it was initially a jazz-only festival, it has since broadened its musical horizons.

Valais

The Romans called the area Vallis Poenina (Upper Rhône Valley), but from 888 onwards, the lands were part of the kingdom of Jurane Burgundy. King Rudolph III of Burgundy gave the lands to the Bishop of Sion in 999, making him Count of the Valais. The count-bishops then struggled to defend their area against the dukes of Savoy so that the Medieval history of the Valais is inextricably linked with that of the diocese of Sion. In contrast to neighbouring Vaud, the Valais people resisted the Protestant Reformation and remained faithful to the Roman Catholic Church. On March 12, 1529, Valais became an associate member of the Swiss Confederation, and in 1628, the Republik der Sieben Zehenden (Republic of the Seven Hands) under the guidance of the prince-bishop of Sion. The bishop remained in power until 1798 when Napoleon's troops invaded the Valais and declared it the République du Valais, incorporated into the Helvetic Republic until 1802, when it became the separate Rhodanic Republic. On 4 August 1815, the Valais finally entered the Swiss Confederation as a canton. Valais is dominated by the wide, glacial Rhône valley, with many side valleys branching off it. These vary from narrow and remote to reasonably populous and popular. The Rhône drains almost the entire canton and flows in the main valley from east to west up to Martigny (through which the Via Francigena runs directly), then at a right angle north to its mouth in Lake Geneva. After the small town of Saint-Maurice (also on your route), the northern banks of the river belong to the Canton of Vaud. Apart from tourism, agriculture is still important today, particularly cattle breeding in the mountains and dairy farming in the plains. Vines also share the hillsides with a large number of orchards and the saffron crocus, from which saffron is gathered.

More in keeping with the guidebook theme, the travellers amongst you will be pleased to know that the Via Francigena route follows one of the most beautiful walks along the lake, but if you are beginning to feel the strain and would welcome an opportunity to cut a few corners, or simply can't resist the chance of a ride on the paddle steamer 'Montreux', check out the times and sailing options: www.swissitalianpaddlesteamers.com

Aigle.....La Burbulei

A hospice for the poor and the sick was established in Aigle in the 14th century and remained in operation until the end of the 18th. In Aigle's western quarters, the Chapel district is centred around a sanctuary, which was allied to the Great-Saint-Bernard hospice. The chapel was demolished during the Reformation.

The Fountain district, so named because of its numerous water sources, is located on the right bank of the Grande-Eau, and today you can still see a covered public washhouse.

St Maurice-en-Valais   La See Maurici

St. Maurice is best known for its Abbaye de Saint-Maurice d'Agaune, situated against a cliff in a picturesque section of the Simplon Pass between Geneva and northern Italy. The abbey is renowned for its connection to stories of the martyrdom of the Theban Legions. Built on the ruins of a 1st Century B.C. Roman shrine to the god Mercury in the Roman staging post of Agaunum, the Basilica of St. Maurice of Agaunum became the centre of a monastery under the patronage of King Sigismund of Burgundy, the first ruler in his dynasty to convert from Arian to Trinitarian Christianity. After being a point of contention and serial ownership over the centuries, Pope Gregory XVI finally gave the abbey its title of See of Bethlehem in Perpetuity in 1840. The abbey has been built and rebuilt over at least fifteen centuries. Excavations on the site have revealed a baptistry dating back to the 4th and 5th centuries, a series of four main churches built over one another dating from the 5th to the 11th century, and crypts built between the 4th and 8th centuries. The church you will see was first built in the 17th century, but the tower is 11th century.

St Maurice

Commander of the all-Christian Theban Legion, revered as the patron saint of the infantry, Saint Maurice is generally believed to have been a soldier who lived near Thebes in Egypt in the 3rd century AD. Legend tells us that Maurice was the leader of the Theban Legion, composed of some 6,600 Christians recruited in Egypt to fight for the Roman Empire in Gaul, serving under Maximian. He was put to death, along with all of his men, in the year 287AD as a punishment for refusing to obey orders to torture and kill fellow Christians in what is now modern-day St Maurice-en-Valais. Saint Maurice is one of the most well-known soldier saints who was celebrated in the Middle Ages. In 961, his remains and those of the men who perished with him were disinterred and reburied with honours at the Cathedral of Magdeburg, where his relics remain to this day.

Martigny

The Gaulish name of the settlement in the 1st century BC was either Octodurus or Octodurum. Octodurus was conquered by the Roman Republic in 57 BC to protect the strategically important pass of Poeninus (now known as the Great St. Bernard pass). A restored Roman amphitheatre, temples, citizen living quarters, and thermal baths can still be seen in Martigny today. An episcopal See was established in Martigny in the 4th century, making the Roman Catholic Diocese of Sion the oldest bishopric in what is now Switzerland. There are no records of the town during the early Medieval period, but in the Middle Ages, it took Martin of Tours as its patron saint and became known by the German name of Martinach. The church of Martigny, presumably at the site of the ancient cathedral, was consecrated to St. Mary in 1177 and to Notre-Dame-des-Champs in 1420. Martigny was placed under the protection of the House of Savoy in 1351. Its citizens were granted a degree of autonomy. Even so, in the 1840s, Martigny was the stage of a confrontation between the liberal-radical Young Switzerland and the conservative Old Switzerland movements, culminating in the Battle at the Trient of 21 May 1844. As a result, the town was split into the independent municipalities of Martigny-Ville, Charrat, Martigny-Bourg and Martigny-Combe, but this was reversed in the 20th century to become the unified community we find today. Martigny is surrounded by vineyards and orchards because the climate is ideal for growing strawberries, apricots, grapes and asparagus. It is also well known for its famous visitors: Rousseau, Goethe, Stendhal and Liszt. Less seriously and culturally, cow fights are held in the Roman amphitheatre during early autumn - a bizarre spectacle not to be missed if you happen to be there at the right time. These poor milkers may not be king of the beasts, but the most belligerent bovines win the prized title - Queen of the Alps. Unlike bullfighting, cows don't kill or seriously hurt anybody, not even one another. Veterinarians file the cows' horns before a fight if they are too sharp, but it is hard to provoke a cow into a fight if it doesn't want to. Perhaps the only living beings to get really excited about all of this are the farmers because the calf of a bell-winner can sell for nearly ten times the going price of an ordinary calf.

St Martin of Tours

Legend has it that San Martino became a monk after serving as a Roman soldier. On a cold rainy day in November, Martino travelled on horseback and came across a poor beggar shivering from the cold. Martino took pity on him and cut his own cloak in half, giving one half to the beggar. The sun came out as soon as Martino set off again, and the temperature became warm. From this, we get the phrase - the Summer of San Martino. That night, Martino dreamt of Jesus wearing his cloak and woke up with his own cloak intact. This sign made him ask for baptism and

to become a Christian. Besides bringing warm November weather, San Martino has many chores as a patron saint of horsemen, horses, tailors, beggars, the poor, injured, barrel makers, winemakers, drunks, cured alcoholics, and last but not least, betrayed husbands.

Orsiéres L Ursiores

At an altitude of 900 metres, Orsières is home to several architectural treasures, the indisputable jewel in the crown being the church and its bell tower. Dedicated to Saint Nicolas, it was built in 1895 on the site of two known former churches: the first built between 1177 and 1296, the second devoted in 1497. Orsiéres is also known for the medicinal and aromatic plants grown on its surrounding slopes, which are used to make herbal and iced teas or to manufacture beauty and healthcare products.

Bourg-st-Pierre XLIX Petrecastel

During the wars of the 1790s, entire armies crossed the pass, and in May 1800, Napoleon led 40,000 troops over it into Italy, consuming on the way 21,724 bottles of wine, a tonne and a half of cheese, 800kg of meat and more. The bill came to a staggering Fr.40,000, but though Napoleon sent an IOU promising, "I will reimburse everything," he ultimately dodged the payment. When President François Mitterrand visited Bourg-st-Pierre, its inhabitants politely reminded him of the outstanding debt but did not ask for a specific sum. In response, a personal representative of Mitterrand's returned, bearing a commemorative plaque and a handwritten letter thanking the village for the hospitality shown to Napoleon. Shortly after, Fr.18,500 was offered as a token gesture of account settling concerning the village's debts and the construction of a swimming pool in Bourg-st-Pierre. French officials said the matter had been resolved in a "warm and friendly way." Mayor Fernand Dorsaz accepted the plaque and letter as symbols of the debt's amicable settlement and declared the matter "closed and settled."

The Alpine Crossing of Hannibal

Some details of Hannibal's crossing of the Alps have been preserved, chiefly by Polybius, who is said to have travelled the route himself. When Hannibal set out, the first to oppose his crossing was a tribelet of the Allobroges, who may have been angered by Hannibal's intervention on behalf of Brancus. This group attacked the rear of Hannibal's column in an ambush, possibly along the Isère at the "gateway to the Alps" (near modern Grenoble) and possibly where the river is at its narrowest, surrounded by high ridges of the Chartreuse and Belledonne massifs. Hannibal took countermeasures, but but lost many men. On the third day, he captured a Gallic town and stole from its stores to provide the army with rations for two or three days. After about four more days of passage along river valleys (very possibly the Isère and Arc rivers, although that is debated) and through increasing elevations, Hannibal was ambushed by hostile Gauls at a "white-rock" place apparently one day's march from the summit. Those unnamed Gauls attacked the baggage animals and rolled heavy stones down from the heights, causing both men and animals to panic and lose their footing on the steep paths. Harassed by these daytime assaults and mistrusting the loyalty of his Gallic guides, Hannibal bivouacked on a large bare rock to cover the passage by night of his horses and pack animals in the gorge below. Then, before dawn, he led the remainder of his force through the narrow gorge entrance, killing the few Gauls who had guarded it and believed Hannibal to be trapped. Mustering his forces at the summit of the Alps, Hannibal remained camped there for several days before his descent into Italy. Polybius makes it clear that the summit of at least 8,000 feet (2,400 metres) itself must have been high enough for snow drifts to persist from the previous winter but the name of the pass was either not known to Polybius and his sources or it was thought not sufficiently important to provide to their mostly Roman readers. Livy, writing 150 years later, sheds no additional light on the matter, but modern historians have posited numerous theories including the low passes at Montgenèvre, The Little St. Bernard, and Mount Cenis, as well as the high passes at Col du Clapier–Savine Coche and Col de la Traversette.

The Great-St-Bernard Pass

"It was high morning, and everyone was full of fear and trembling. Through holy prayer, we were preparing to face menacing death…"

Written by a Belgian abbot in 1129.

The Great St Bernard Pass is the most ancient route through the Western Alps, crossing at 2,473 metres and one of the highest Alpine frontier passes. Named after Saint Bernard of Menthon, who founded a hospice at its summit in the 11th century, the Great-St-Bernard Pass has been in use since the Bronze Age, with tribes and armies tramping their way to and fro for millennia since. In 390 BC, a Gaulish army crossed to defeat Rome, and from the earliest times, ordinary people used the pass to trade goods between northern Europe and Italy. Hannibal's famous crossing of the Alps in 217 BC is indelibly associated with the Great Saint Bernard pass, and (though there's little actual evidence of it actually having taken place) in the 1930s, the fabulously eccentric American travel writer Richard Halliburton rode his elephant over the pass to re-enact the journey. Sadly, the poor beast suffered from altitude sickness and stalled on the summit. In 57 BC, Julius Caesar crossed the Summa Poenina, as it was known then, to conquer the pagan peoples of Martigny, who worshipped the Celtic god Poenn. Shortly after, Emperor Augustus built a road across the pass and left a temple to Jupiter

on the summit, which subsequently lent its name to the area (Mons Iovis, or Mont Joux). Unfortunately, the temple was sacked with the fall of Rome, but since the great and the good continued to tramp the road, it is assumed that refuge may have remained on the pass. Pope Stephen II crossed in November 753 to meet with Pepin the Short. At that point, Deeply concerned by the disruption caused to merchants and pilgrims Europe-wide, King Canute of Denmark took King Rudolf III of Burgundy to one side to have a quiet word. As a result, the heathens were ejected, and the archdeacon of Aosta, one Bernard of Menthon (who had spent years tending to travellers coming down off the pass stripped of all their belongings), was given permission to oversee the construction of the hospice. Bernard himself travelled around the area, spreading the word of God and was beatified after he died in 1080. Pope Pius XI confirmed him as Patron Saint of the Alps in 1923. The hospice immediately became a welcome safety point on an extremely dangerous route, attracting favours and gifts from royal and noble households. Throughout the Middle Ages, the hospice provided free shelter and food to pilgrims, clerics and travellers, many crossing to and from Rome. By 1817, some 20,000 people had been using the road annually.

The hospice on the pass is still used by Augustinian monks who, with their St. Bernard dogs, provide services to travellers. When you finally reach the summit of the Great St Bernard Pass, the first building you will see is the Combe de Morte, a charnel house where the corpses of those who did not make it over the pass were mummified by the cold. But don't worry, it is no longer in use. Next, look for the sign informing travellers that they are 2473 metres up - an obligatory photo stop. Then, head to the hostel or hotel and take a much-needed  shower. After that, if you still have sufficient energy, visit the St. Bernard Dog Museum, an important part of the Great St Bernard Pass history. Probably descended from mastiff-like dogs, the St Bernard dogs were brought to the hospice in the late 17th century and remain loyal companions to the monks living there. The name St. Bernard was dedicated to Bernard of Menthon. The most famous dog was Barry, who reportedly saved between forty and one hundred lives. There is a monument to Barry in the Cimetiére des Chiens, and his body is preserved in the Natural History Museum in Berne.

Next stop, Italy!!

www.ingramcontent.com/pod-product-compliance
Lightning Source LLC
LaVergne TN
LVHW020139080526
838202LV00048B/3973